FINDING THE FORCE:

10 Tips and Trips on Dying

COURTNI "STARHEART" HALE

FINDING THE FORCE 1:

FINDING THE FORCE 1
Table of Contents

PROLOGUE — 5
CHAPTER ONE — 8
 Patricio Dominguez
 TRIP 1: DREAM OF THE VILLAGE
CHAPTER TWO — 33
 Roger Nelson
 TRIP 2: DREAM OF THE FLYING JAGUAR
CHAPTER THREE — 46
 John Major Jenkins
 TRIP 3: DREAM OF THE ESCAPE OF THE TRIBE
CHAPTER FOUR — 62
 Joseph Chilton Pearce
 TRIP 4: DREAM OF THE MELTING METROPOLIS
CHAPTER FIVE
 Dr. Quantum — 80
 TRIP 5: DREAM OF THE HOWLING WOLF MAN
CHAPTER SIX
 Jose and Miguel Ruiz — 94
 TRIP 6: DREAM OF THE BUTTERFLY LOTUS
CHAPTER SEVEN — 111
 Masaru Emoto
 TRIP 7: DREAM OF THE TURTLE LODGE
 CHAPTER EIGHT
 Divine Consciousness — 122
TRIP 8: DREAM OF THE "HIT" MEN

FINDING THE FORCE 1:

PROLOGUE

Everything that happened in this novel is true. People will believe what sounds true to them, and it will be different for each person. Just like love means something different to everyone even though it's the same word.

When I was dying, or mostly dead (in the Spirit World) I didn't know exactly what was happening, but more than anything I wanted to leave behind something that made sense. Something for my kids, because I was afraid I wouldn't be around when they grew up, and because I felt so much Love in my heart, more than any other time, as I was transitioning into the Spirit World, or Dying, in this world.

"Ten Tips and Trips While Dying" will give you just that: 10 important pieces of information I learned from world renowned experts as I was grasping for some thread of reality, near death. We are inextricably intertwined by an all pervasive web of light, and the subject of this book is my personal exploration of Universal Love, which is what we are left with, or what we are lacking when we transition out of our bodies.

This more mystical thinking is balanced with interviews with experts in consciousness, physics, shamanism, meditation and neurology. It is also a book about my descent into madness, I suppose, or my direct noncompliance with societal norms in order to explore both science and shamanism.

When this book began, I did not know it, but I was being exposed to *e coli* bacteria in my drinking water, bathing water, and in the stream that I often bathed in. It took many years to figure it out, and it is a miracle I survived. Perhaps that inner struggle with death is what provided for my strangely vivid dreams. But they never stopped, so I am not sure.

FINDING THE FORCE 1

What I am sure about is that I painted, researched, interviewed and did all I could to understand what was going on when my normal reality melted away before my eyes. And in a way, at least now, it all makes sense.

The format of this book is unconventional. There are two modes. *One is at the beginning of each chapter, where I share my adventures and interviews, and one is at the end, which are the "Trips" or the Dream Sequences.* You'll also find a TIP at the end of the Chapter, which is the very short kernel of wisdom from that Interview. Generally only my dreams and my thoughts are in italics.

The other mode is normal waking reality, my research as a writer, shaped by the dreams, visions and much intuition. There are watercolor illustrations of my dreams, which have taken me a long time to understand and were often explained by my visits with the interviewees.

This journey of Love coming home began with my journey as a mother. I wanted very much to know more about our world, and if it's possible for us to become something greater than what we are right now. I didn't know that my entire way of thinking had to be torn down before I could understand the answers to my questions. Nevertheless, something answered in the best way it could. I didn't even understand the answers sometimes because I had to learn to speak the language of Spirit.

There is a perennial language, sometimes called the Language of the Birds, which is a little different for everyone, but it can be learned. It forms a basis for communication on a symbolic level, beyond intellect, reason and words.

For more than two years, I had a recurring and very lucid dream that I was in a place where we had all come to live together in a community. Not a hippie commune, but a very refined, elegant community where professionals, activists and teachers were sharing life in communal areas

FINDING THE FORCE 1:

while owning quarters in their own space. There was food growing everywhere, natural architecture and design, and lots of light.

In these dreams, the distinguishing feature was always a sense of beautiful peace. In fact, I asked repeatedly if I was dead, and was told no. There was a daughter in the dreams who was not born yet, and she was able to guide me from that place, both there and in waking reality. She seemed to believe that if she was born, there was a good chance that I could find the thread of reality that we inhabited together in the dreamtime.

I essentially lost my mind over these dreams. It was so beautiful that I was willing to let go of everything I ever had in order to find that place. Life wasn't the same without that light.

So many synchronicities popped up each day, I felt totally sure that I was being guided and supported. In fact, at times, supernaturally so.

There is no way to prove scientifically that what I have detailed for you here in this book is *true*.

But there is scientific evidence in this book to demonstrate that it is *possible*. Publishers have been unable to categorize it. Fiction? Non-fiction? Auto-biography? Shamanism? Science fiction??

Decide for yourself. I hope you enjoy it because it has been a hard journey to prove to myself that anything is possible if we dream it. If I could have dreamed any dream though, it would have been this one. I am on a thread of life that is full of Love, and I hope I can somehow express in words how that is to swim that long journey home.

There are many paths to consciousness, to happiness, maybe even enlightenment. What is yours? Will our paths cross and interweave on the tapestry of time? Will this book change the way you see things? Maybe your inner voice will seem louder.

Maybe you will listen carefully to your dreams.

Courtni "StarHeart" Hale
Albuquerque, NM
1/3/2017

CHAPTER ONE

Patricio Dominguez

Nothing lasts forever.
No one lives forever.
Keep that in mind, and Love.
          -Rumi

FINDING THE FORCE 1:

Albuquerque, NM, March 2004

Driving down the highway from Santa Fe to Albuquerque wasn't one of the greatest scenic routes in New Mexico, but to me, it was one of those moments I will never forget.

When the sun burst forth before me and those first rays emerged over the mesa tops, I thought this was what the first day looked like.

Unlike anywhere with forests and trees, in New Mexico, nothing filters the light of the sun. At one given moment, the sun reaches the top of the mountains and then, boom! The light spills fully out over the mountains like liquid gold, touching every crevasse and arroyo of the unique desert formations. For an artist, it is spectacular, since the colors change with every heartbeat, shifting in bronzes, pinks and purples and gold. If our planet were a woman, then this place would be the soft, smooth, sun-bronzed belly of Mother Earth. The colors made me want to return to a sweet slumber.

But instead there I was, drinking some coffee, driving along with my tiny son in the back seat, munching on waffles and babbling. I had just arrived from New York two nights before, and was still trying to get my bearings.

I was on my way to interview Don Patricio Dominguez, who had agreed to grant me an hour to speak and see where things went. I had explained that I was writing a book on sustainable development, and the Indigenous point of view on what kind of changes ought to be made to bring humanity back into harmony with our planet.

It didn't seem like the phone was the best moment to mention to him that I was having really weird dreams of a place called World Womb, and a daughter that hadn't been born.

I had called and made arrangements from New York. He had said that the last interview he had done was with the writers of a book on *The Mystery of the Crystal Skulls*, and that it had lasted over the course of days as they followed him about. He had also said that he didn't think he had it in him to do that again, and that he had become more of an administrator than an active spiritual leader.

What he didn't mention then was that he had eventually received hundreds of letters from around the world, as well as phone calls, which he answered. Those were just from *The Mystery of the Crystal Skulls*.

When the *Celestine Prophecy* came out though, people had started actually looking for him physically, crazed by the thought of gaining the Tenth Insight. Even though he had nothing to do with the book...

He was horrified. *The Celestine Prophecy* was a made-up story trying to convey some aspects of truth, without really telling the whole story. But it was a story that sold, and really influenced a lot of people's lives, and they were temporarily crazed by the innate desire to complete the circle, and come to a higher truth. He couldn't believe that all those calls in the middle of the night, all those drive-bys and letters had all been about a made-up story.

I guess he was relieved when he heard over the phone that I was writing a true story, and doing research. I told him that I didn't have to use his name, and then he really relaxed. No more drive-bys or phone calls.

When I arrived Patricio Dominguez greeted me and invited us in. He didn't look upset that I came with a baby in tow, the way people are in New York. They think you can't be serious about an interview if a baby is with you. Decent people put those in day care.

Looking around the room, there were objects piled up everywhere in stacks, as well as at least two fully rigged computers with all their accoutrement, and things hanging from the walls everywhere too.

Dominguez referred to himself as the *Electric Indian*, and he wasn't joking. There was a lot of technological gadgets and stuff around, but somehow there was an organic feeling to the arrangement. Maybe it was like the difference between a pruned garden and a field of wildflowers. It was full of life everywhere.

A key piece to understanding Patricio's appeal to the public as an expert on Indigenous Culture is that he wasn't only trained in

FINDING THE FORCE 1:

Traditional ways, he was also an engineer with a master's degree, trained in traditional Western society.

He had said in his interview in *The Mystery of the Crystal Skulls* that he had his 'foot in both worlds' and was like a conduit for information to flow back and forth between dissimilar ways of seeing the world.

Looking at his home, there certainly wasn't much that would indicate that a shaman lived there. Just a picture of Patricio gazing out over the side of a cliff face in the jungle somewhere, playing flute…

Turning towards him, I could see how dark his eyes were, how smooth his skin. He must have been at least sixty, and looked younger than me in many ways. His black hair was thick and straight, not a strand of gray visible, and not a wrinkle in sight, except some laugh lines when he smiled. He looked impossibly young.

Except the eyes.

The eyes were another story. Even though he had brown eyes, they had an unusual swirling effect that gave the onlooker the impression that they were held unspoken secrets. Not secrets really, but knowledge, and depth. Don Patricio looked like another species of human being in fact, unearthly, but part of the very earth at once, like a rock mesa.

I found myself under his aware gaze just wanting to confess the dream right up front, and be done with it. Still, I was supposed to be a professional, and ask serious questions for background research. Plus, I thought it would sound a little odd to show up at someone's door because an unborn daughter in the future had told me to paint some poppies and bring the painting to a stranger across the country.

So, naturally I found myself asking him about something less personal, hoping that over the course of time we might get to know each other and be able to talk freely. Essentially my research and why Arusha was contacting me were one and the same.

2012.

Better yet, Beyond 2012.

Many people were discussing the meaning and implications of the end of the Mayan calendar in 2012. Some said it would be a time of spiritual changes, some said there would be catastrophic natural disasters. I knew that a large part of the reason why, in my dreams, we had made World Womb was because we couldn't survive any longer in modern society, and had seceded, so to speak.

The only way I could really keep my sanity and also pursue what my unborn daughter was saying was to essentially accept that something extraordinary is possible. And that opens the doors to a lot of things.

One of the topics that kept popping up was the Dreamtime.

The Dreamtime is essentially an-out-o- the-physical state or place that is both past and future, possibilities and potentials, as well as spirit. From there one can access many things that are extraordinary, and I believe that was where I was going. I was starting to get sick from the exhaustion though of not sleeping properly, and instead going to this other state, where I was awake in a different place. What I really needed to know was just what was possible in the shamanic world, and what was going on from Dominguez's point of view.

The 2012 topic was now least strange of my panel of questions.

Funny how relative life is. I was now trying to analyze the comparative strangeness of two different tracks of questions, and the *least strange* was the one on Mayan prophecies about the end of our civilization in a couple years.

Or the end of the world as we know it.

"Should we get started?" prompted Dominguez after everyone had settled in

I took a deep breath and dove in.

"Sure. I guess the point of departure for the book is the coming planetary changes in 2012 and the Indigenous traditions about it."

Dominguez didn't look too happy, but he certainly knew what I was talking about. It was odd because until that moment, I had been the only person I knew who put any stock into the Maya prophecies about changes coming in 2012. He thought it was old news.

"Look, I really feel that has been so well covered that it's hardly worth revisiting."

"But it's essentially the point of departure for what we're talking about," I said as I took a deep breath and settled back in, continuing to look at him.

FINDING THE FORCE 1:

I have noticed that in these cases in life, he who talks first loses, and I hadn't come to Albuquerque from New York to lose on the first question.

We sat there and looked at one another. It got very quiet. Finally he sighed and began to speak.

"Well, look," he said turning to his computer.

Clicking on a few buttons, he pulled up an interview with a lady named Camida from the Wompanoag Tribe in the Northeast who spoke about visions of her family crossing a long distance on foot, alongside a deeply worn track in the dirt. She said people were tired and taking just what they could carry on their backs. The sky was dark and they were headed to a safe place together. The interview went on for some ten minutes, and then he turned to look at me.

He played the video, but a little annoyed, as if to say to me,

Is this seriously the best you can do?

Since I was still the only person I knew socially (outside of my research) who put stock in this 2012 prophecy, I guess I better explain some. By now most people know, but still there seems to be a lot of misinformation about what's supposed to happen.

The bottom line is that our planet moves through cycles because of the wobble in its axial revolutions, which causes the constellations to shift across the sky over very long periods of time. The Ancients used this movement to track the larger motions of time, and to try to understand the contour of space-time from a higher perspective. This perspective deals with huge amounts of time, namely 26 thousand years at a time.

According to the Ancients, especially the Maya and several other peoples around the globe, to mark every 26,000 year cycle, the planet would experience some degree of changes. The changes in the past had included events such as the Great Flood, the extinction of the dinosaurs, possibly shifting tectonic plates and allegedly a shift in the quality of light coming from the sun.

Simply put, at certain points in her life cycles Mother Earth would roll over in her sleep, and shift into a more comfortable position. Especially at those fragile transitional points, the world was subject to some disruption and needed to be in harmony with itself inside and out.

FINDING THE FORCE 1

If the planet was getting ready to roll over in her sleep, and start a new dream, what was she going to be dreaming of?

It seemed ridiculous to me I when I first began reading about it. As the years went on though, I found more and more compelling evidence to support these theories, from a wide variety of sources, scientific and esoteric alike.

Throughout the course of this book we will revisit the subject of 2012 while also building the case for human advancement to a more caring and inclusive global society, even in the absence of evidence to validate changing energies around 2012.

Leading-edge science and Ancient Traditions have a great deal in common though. In many cases, Indigenous or ancient spiritual cosmology provides the best explanation for the wacky world of quantum physics and other modern discoveries that we will touch lightly upon.

But how had these spiritual people all over the world understood this thousands of years before Western empirical "science" developed? What kind of life were they leading that they were a part of the larger expanses of the universe while being in a human body?

Like he had sensed what I was getting after, Don Patricio introduced a related piece of the puzzle.

He pulled up a website about the Hopi Stone Prophecies.

He explained that the Hopi, not unlike other people around the world who had maintained their original instructions and subsequent prophecies, were determined to live apart from modern society, on a handful of mesas in the middle of the desert. Even the Spanish conquistadors gave up the idea by the time they marched out there. So the Hopi hadn't lost of changed too much in the past five thousand years, at least. And this was a reproduction of one of their stone tablets (like Moses).

It was a basic, but very descriptive drawing. There was a carving in dark lines of stick figures moving around between some straight and wavy lines. Like many other instances, to the untrained eye, it didn't appear like much. As Don Patricio read from the web page, things became still more clear...

FINDING THE FORCE 1:

"Prophecy Rock is a petroglyph on the Hopi Reservation in Arizona that describes the life path of our world. It represents the prophecy connected with the return of the White Brother to the land, who should be carrying a cross within a sacred circle. If, however, he happened to return with only the cross and no circle, this could be the beginning of the Great Purification that would bring about the end of the world. The current day Hopi believe that the White Brother first returned to the land in the form of the Spanish invaders in the 1500's, who were carrying the cross but no sacred circle (they came as enemies rather than friends). Since that time, according to Hopi beliefs, we have been approaching the end of the world as we know it.

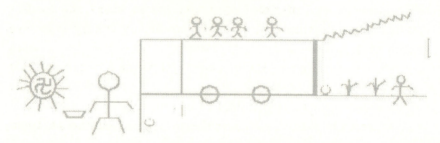

The lower left hand corner depicts the Great Spirit holding the reed through which the people traveled to enter the fourth world.

The people had the choice of taking either of two paths: the upper horizontal line is the materialistic path, while the lower line is the spiritual path. The first vertical line (just before the circles) represents the moment that the white people returned to Hopi land. (In the actual petroglyph, the people on the top line are not connected with their heads, which indicates their dissociation from their spirituality and the Creator.) The first two circles represent World War I and II. The vertical line following the two wars is the last chance that the people on the top line (people in our modern culture) could return to the spiritual path and therefore survive to enter the joy and abundance of the fifth world. The materialistic path then becomes jagged and gradually fades away.

The Hopi believe that humanity is now almost at the point of the Great Purification that will mark the end of the fourth world, represented

FINDING THE FORCE 1

by the third circle, and entrance into the fifth. The prophecies also say that just before the purification comes, there will be signs such as: trees dying, major climate changes, land sinking and rising, and the appearance of a blue star that is not yet visible."

When he finished, things grew quiet once again. I couldn't help but feel like I should plead for more assistance, for more help from those who understood these changes.

I had completely suspended any disbelief in these matters.

"But don't we have the responsibility to others to share this information and to help to heal the planet?" I really still wasn't able to accept that this kind of global disruption was imminent, nor for that matter, that my daughter in some future potentiality was trying to save me.

"Yes, sure we do. But you can't tell people how to live," said Dominguez.

"What do you mean?" I asked.

"Well, for example, the Hopi went to the UN four times to try to speak to the people of the world," he stated.

"And?"

"Oh, they gave them about ten minutes," Patricio said as he started to laugh again.

"What??" I had to laugh too, because of the sheer absurdity of the thing.

"Yeah, they packed their things and went, at their own expense, four times to knock on the "Mica doors," in accordance with their legends and traditions.

It was foreseen that they would fulfill their responsibility to their brothers by telling them four times officially that they should cease and desist from their mode of existence because it was harmful and devastating to the planet, and to one another. I'll read you some of the speech that was delivered:

"Nature itself does not speak with a voice that we can easily understand. Neither can the animals and birds we are threatening with extinction talk to us. Who in this world can speak for nature and the spiritual energy that creates and flows through all life? In every

FINDING THE FORCE 1:

continent are human beings who are like you but who have not separated themselves from the land and from nature. It is through their voice that Nature can speak to us. You have heard those voices and many messages from the four corners of the world today. I have studied comparative religion and I think in your own nations and cultures you have knowledge of the consequences of living out of balance with nature and spirit.

The native peoples of the world have seen and spoken to you about the destruction of their lives and homelands, the ruination of nature and the desecration of their sacred sites. It is time the United Nations used its rules to investigate these occurrences and stop them now."

Don Patricio sat there and looked at me like I should be drawing my own conclusions.

"I take it no one listened."

"Well, let's have a look here at the Epilogue:

The night before the presentations of the native people from around the world to the General Assembly, there was a total eclipse of the moon over New York City and the sky was clear. The evening after the presentation by Mr. Banyacya and the other native spokespersons, heavy rain and strong wind began. The weathermen had been calling for a snowstorm but what came the following day were the worst floods in New York's memory. Major highways were washed away by the sea and the United Nations itself experienced flooding of its lower sub floors, forcing a shutdown of its heating and air conditioning and all personnel were dismissed at three o'clock.

In the ground floor meeting room, where on December 11, native peoples were meeting representatives of various UN agencies; Thomas Banyacya spontaneously called on all the participants, including UN officials, to form a great circle. All the Elders were in the center and Thomas called in some non-native people as well. Each silently said a prayer. The forming of the circle of unity of all people from the four corners of the Earth was more than just a symbolic act. One participant said she had never felt herself to be in such a safe place. Later, several people present noted that no further storm damage occurred in Manhattan and that the storm itself abated that afternoon."

"That's unbelievable. And that was back in December of 1992?"
"Yes, towards the beginning of the cycle of Changes. December 26 2012 marks the peak of the curve. Right now we are well into the consequences of having ignored these warnings. It's essentially tóo late to do anything but prepare for the upcoming Changes and ride them out."

"But wait; looking at the Prophecy Stone, can't we do something to create another line that connects us to the earth again? Isn't it at least possible?" I sat staring at the prophecies of the Hopi Stone. I tried hard to visualize a straight line coming down where some people could exit the top block before all those squiggly lines carried them off to their appointed moment of destruction. I looked down at my little baby and felt panicky. And then some.

What about the innocent children and peoples all over the world who have done no wrong?

"Sure, in theory, at least, anything is possible, "replied Dominguez.

"But not likely?"

"The prophecy is what it is. From whatever place, the seers saw what they saw. It represents probabilities. But it is highly likely that it is too late now."

Perhaps what was most upsetting was that there was not a hint of doubt in his demeanor about the subject matter.

I had previously only heard New Age people talking about the "Changes" like it was a schoolyard secret. Many people seemed to think that it was a remote possibility, a possibility from which they were safeguarded by their secret knowledge of it.

Still though, none of the New Age followers I had met had undertaken the real business of making a place where people would have the chance to see there was an alternative.

It's hard to convince people they should be one with the Earth when they were busy watching horror and violence on the news, and charging up their credit card bills.

We didn't need to go back to the Dark Ages; we needed to move forward into the Light Ages.

FINDING THE FORCE 1:

Society had exceeded the bounds where it was probable that anyone could hear the heartbeat of the Earth enough to be willing to make the drastic changes that would be required to come back into harmony.

"OK, assuming that these changes are coming, and assuming that their intensity will be determined by our consciousness as humans, what is going to be good technology to take along with us through the changes?"

"Technology? We are going to be taking what's on our backs, as the woman in the interview said." Don Patricio gestured to the computer, offering to replay the interview for me since I had apparently missed the point.

I laughed and shook my head 'no'.

At that point I saw my portfolio and thought it might be a good moment to ask Dominguez about the Poppy painting.

Looking at the Poppies, I think he began to sense what was going on. I told him that I had had a dream where I was shown this painting and told to come and see him.

"Interesting," he commented without continuing.

"What's interesting about it?" I pursued him.

"Well, the poppies, the raven, the stairway leading up to the window. The configuration of stars and moon in the picture. The woman looking straight at you, looking right back. She is there, but she is really not. There are some profound symbols working here that would be difficult to explain without a lot of training."

I was pleased that he was seeing the same type of things I was. I showed him some other paintings, and inquired about what might be going on.

"It looks as if maybe during your pregnancy, with all the hormones perhaps that a door got opened up in your mind. Your consciousness has expanded to include things that it was not formerly open to," he remarked as he continued to look at the paintings. Then he just put them away.

When he was done, he was done, and no amount of questioning was going to provide more answers. We returned to our previous conversation, a little more lighthearted than before.

I was beginning to relax, and understand that although this was a person to be respected and treated with reverence, he was still just like the rest of us human beings in many senses.

He had a great sense of humor, and when he laughed he would throw his head back and his eyes twinkled.

Perhaps that had been the best part of all.

That funny laugh.

"So, isn't there anything we can do right now to prepare for these changes coming?" I was bound and determined to find out what I could from him about how I should design this community. In fact, I was trying to pick his brain to see if he really might know my daughter in some future potentiality.

Anything was possible he had said.

"Well, let me make a phone call and check on something." Throughout the meeting the phone had been ringing, and though he had said it was his one day to take care of business around the house for his family, it seemed that he was completely engaged in some unknown business he was administrating.

About a dozen calls from other spiritual leaders and friends had come through where he was speaking about classes, engagements and plans for something. Now he was on another call, to an assistant, talking about plans.

"Oh, so you aren't going to be able to help out today? A doctor's appointment? Oh, OK, don't worry. I have someone here who may be able to help." He smiled about the person's polite refusal to engage in whatever project he had planned for them. Apparently it wasn't too appealing.

He turned to look at Adrian and me with that same smile. I felt something unpleasant might be coming. We walked outside and the shaman pointed to some tools.

"Well, since you are interested in useful technology, I think I can give you a better idea about what you might need," said Dominguez, as he handed me a shovel.

He must have thought it was really funny to see my mouth drop when I realized what he was driving at. A shovel and some mud were

FINDING THE FORCE 1:

what he considered useful technology! I didn't mind digging and shoveling, so that was no issue. It was just the shock value of entering his reality, where the only useful tools were going to be mud brick and shovels.

"Are you kidding? That's great!" I was relieved and delighted that he was going to include my in something. Maybe it was going to be something big, something I could include in my novel, and would help me to build a community. I could hardly wait to see what this man was going to show me!

"You don't mind a little bit of work do you?"

"No, no not at all. It's the least I can do,"

"OK then. Off we go."

As we began to tour the yard, I could see that there were a couple of special features. He had a sweat lodge in the back corner, and took us over to show it to us. It was a fairly small sweat lodge, probably big enough for a half dozen people or so.

To the other side, and much larger, was another structure, also about halfway underground, like the sweat lodge. As my eyes adjusted to the bright mid afternoon sun, I realized that this must be some kind of ceremonial structure.

What kind of thing could it be that he was building?

"This is our Kiva here." Dominguez guided us down the straight dirt ramp that led into the round building. It was unfinished as yet, and covered with plastic. Inside I could see that it was spacious, with a clay chimenea-style fireplace in the middle.

"I have constructed it all naturally, with the help of my Community. Look, see, the door here is made from wood, the fireplace in the center is natural, and the walls have been made from the soil right here. It's all naturally made, almost like in the old days."

I couldn't believe my good fortune. Here I was standing in the middle of a Kiva, made by hand naturally, so much like the one in my dream that it was bone chilling. Just different proportions, and I could be standing in the place called World Womb in my dreams.

As we went outside, Patricio was gathering tools to begin work.

"My helper today can't show up, so I thought that I would see if you wanted to help me finish the south wall," and he pointed to the area outside where light had been entering into the dark womb-like Kiva inside.

"Sure no problem! I'll just grab the baby carrier and see if the baby will hang out while we work," and I went to the rental car where the baby carrier was laying on the seat.

When I returned to the yard, Dominguez was digging a hole with a shovel, and shifting water around in it to make mud.

"*This* is useful technology..." and he looked up and smiled a big wide grin. I knew that he thought this was pretty funny, but so did I.

I loved working with earth, and there was nothing I liked more than the idea of working with another person to build something useful. In everyday life I always felt that I was doing things that were meaningless in some way, dictated by a societal construct that was not of my choosing.

This, on the other hand, was useful, and meaningful.

We worked together for a few hours before we went inside to have lunch. By the end of the day we had finished that part of the wall.

Baby Adrian had played and played in the dirt, and with the water, with one special tile in particular, looking around everywhere in amazement. I wondered what he was seeing, because it is said that babies see things that even small children have long forgotten how to see. They begin to focus in on the things that they see us looking at, which limits their abilities substantially. They do come into this world, though, with limitless possibilities.

As we went inside to finish the interview, the baby kept on pointing at things in the corner of the patio. He wasn't pointing at anything stationary or visible though, and his tiny little finger kept moving around to follow something that I couldn't see. He was gesturing frantically asking me what he saw flying around.

Dat? Dat? Dat?

I didn't see anything at all.

"What is he pointing at?" I asked Patricio, now more comfortable with speaking freely.

"Oh, uh, I don't know. Could be pretty much anything around here. Could be a lot of things," he said as he started to grin, and then to laugh until he burst into peels of laughter.

FINDING THE FORCE 1:

"Dat! Dat! Dat!" baby kept insisting, causing us to laugh louder and harder still. I felt years of tension and worry melt away. We laughed harder as the baby's finger kept swooping around pointing to objects invisible to me.

Returning inside at nearly dark, the shaman was ready to wrap things up.

"Is there anything else we haven't covered?"

"Well, a couple of things," I replied. "I wanted to know what you think are the keys to building a proper community that would not only do well through the Earth Changes, but also afterwards, in the spirit of the way we are really meant to live."

"That's not easy, you know. So much goes into it," he replied.

"Well, how many people for example? What kinds of people and how could it be structured?"

"See, that's the problem. I think that maybe each family has to learn to provide what they can for themselves from the earth, or learn to do without."

"That doesn't provide for much though. Couldn't we all learn to cooperate and make a better way?"

"See, that's also the problem with things. A person's perception of things is what determines their experience. For example, the Maya legends say that this time now is the Thirteen Hells, and that we will be entering into the time of the Nine Heavens. But not everyone might have that same experience. Maybe the Maya think it would be great if we could all shovel mud together nicely, but most people think that it would really be Hell! The Thirteen Heavens may not be Heaven for everyone.

"So you're saying "Attitude is everything."

"Yeah, more like "Perception is Reality," he replied.

"And so the Maya really are time jumpers then?"

"That's what they say."

"And do you have any experience that would back that up as a possibility?" I asked him.

"Yeah sure, but not everyone can just pop in and out of this reality. Part of the reason that I am not so concerned about the Changes

FINDING THE FORCE 1

and what is going to happen is that I can just pop in and out and watch the show from the higher seats in the theater."

"Well then why did the Hopi bother at all to talk to the UN? And what about everybody else? What makes you sure that you deserve to live and we all deserve to die?"

"It was part of their prophecy, so the Hopi went to carry the message they were told to. But not being attached to the results. And in a way they were trying to save their own tails. It would certainly be better for everyone if the planet didn't go through so much upheaval. But as it is they have packed it in. They no longer wish to have any contact with the Western world. They are staying at the place where I just got back from, mentally."

"What do you mean," I asked him, curious about his state of mind in the face of these Changes.

"Well, I just got disgusted with the world for a long time, and wasn't going to help anybody with anything. Just about a month ago I came back around though, and have started an organization to help to spread the traditional Native American teachings and technology that will be helpful to people."

"You're going to teach people about shamanism," I asked, hopeful of finding a way to dodge the upcoming bullets as well.

"No, no, there isn't time for that. Even if I wanted to teach anyone, we start at age five and train until we're thirty, about. There's no time left for that. The Changes are coming too soon, and anyhow, that isn't the point," he remarked. Continuing on he clarified his thoughts.

"What I can teach people about is useful things like how to plant and harvest in the traditional ways. How to use plants for healing things like the common cold," he said as he printed out a piece of information on the organization he had begun.

"You see, I ended up having to leave the practice of healing because I am essentially the only one in this group who has the ability to move around in the modern world well. These other people just don't know what to do, and probably don't want to know, for very good reasons. But I think there are some people out there who may deserve to have this information," he ended as he handed me the piece of paper.

FINDING THE FORCE 1:

The organization he had started was called INTK – the Institute for Native and Traditional Knowledge. Just as he said, the purpose was to share knowledge for anyone who was willing to respect Indigenous values and work in a traditional setting, and classes were starting almost immediately. He wasn't wasting any time at all.

Dominquez continued speaking:

"Look, I think that the Tower of Babel was in fact an allegory for what happens to mankind when we stop being able to do for ourselves together in harmony with the Earth and each other. We get too big for our britches. In a tribe it would be like a situation where the arrow makers start thinking they are more important than the hide tanners, or the men start thinking they are more important than the women because they are hunting and women are just cooking and tending the family.

Everyone's role has to be seen as equal and meaningful in order for us all to work in harmony. But you can't tell people how to live, or try to force them.

The Tower of Babel was the same thing. Maybe the language problem was a metaphor.

Maybe the people who were working as engineers began to think their role was better or more crucial than that of the stone layers, and stopped being able to understand things from their point of view. Maybe the whole story was a lesson meaning that, when society gets too tall, it becomes top-heavy and out of proportion in using only reason and technology.

When man starts to think himself godlike in his technological advances, and that he no longer needs Mother Earth, or that each person is more important than the next, that is the moment of imminent collapse, like when Babel fell.

That is where we are right now, Changes or no Changes in 2012. Maybe if enough people become conscious that it seems like it's worthwhile, then things can change," he concluded.

We were getting ready to leave after that last allegory, but before I did I had to ask Dominguez about my dream.

I explained that the Poppy painting had really come from a dream of an eco-community, and that my future unborn daughter had urged me to paint it, and bring it to him.

Further, I explained that it was this was the start of a series of interviews that would culminate in a novel making make it possible to create a community called "World Womb."

At the end of my explanation, I waited for a reaction, and then added,

"My daughter also communicated that, if I didn't do all this just as it was told, that she would never get born and World Womb would never happen," I said and waited.

Patricio looked away for a moment and thought. As he did I finally noticed the date on the document he had handed my about his organization.

I shuddered.

The date of creation of his document was the same date as when I had first had the dream in Rochester that had brought my here. Before he could answer, I pointed out the correlation between the two dates and asked,

"So we are all one after all?"

He smiled and nodded his head in ascent and said,

"Yes, most surely. But even if I could tell you the secret of life, I couldn't make you live that way. A person's own perception is their reality, and it's their right to have whatever perception they choose."

"But you did tell me the secret of life! A number of times today, and you just said it again," I retorted. He just laughed again.

As I was putting my things together to get ready to leave, I remembered that I had cut him off before he could comment on the dream about World Womb and Arusha. He had never remarked what he thought of a not as yet born daughter leading me to him.

"So, what did you think about the dream after all?" I asked walking through the door. His eyes twinkled again when he replied.

"Smart girl," he said.

And that was all.

FINDING THE FORCE 1:

TRIP 1: DREAM OF THE VILLAGE
Rochester, NY February 12, 2004

In the dream I could see a woman walking across a field of snow, silhouetted by the moonlight above. It was a big round full moon, and she was wearing snowshoes and a thick woolen cape that covered my head. We were walking towards a round wooden lodge and stopped for a moment to gaze at the light coming through the window.

Though she was not me, I could see through her eyes as if she were. Was that my own hair brushing against her cheek? I saw the same thing she looked at, like we were one mind and one thought together, but two bodies in two places.

We were looking at the spurts of snowflakes shifting down from the roof and spinning into and out of the window's light. The snowflakes dropped from their invisibility in the darkness and shimmered for a moment through the yellow light. Then, falling slowly and dancing, the snowflakes disappeared once again.

That reminds me of something, we thought. I guess we were both momentarily hypnotized. Then we moved to the door, and I saw the inside of the large round building.

It was full of people, and they apparently all knew the woman who came in. They called her Arusha and I could feel that there was a sincere warmth and affection coming from them. It was like I knew what they were feeling in the dream.

They loved us.

We loved them.

Strangely enough, I split away from Arusha's vision into my own. I was there, myself, sitting at a big table. I looked around to see where I was and found that I knew everyone. It didn't seem strange in the dream. I had more children than I had thought to have.

Then I also knew that the woman whose eyes I had seen through outside was my daughter. I remember thinking I did not have a daughter.

FINDING THE FORCE 1

I saw someone next who I knew very well, a man with straight black hair twisted into a ponytail. He was fascinating. I could see his hair shining in the light, and I knew that he was an Elder, our Shaman.

Tatti. But that wasn't a very serious name!

As he was talking to the people in the lodge it got quiet. There were new people who had just arrived and they were looking really beaten down, emaciated. They looked barely alive, in all the senses of the words.

It was a Dream of a Village.

The shaman was welcoming them, and trying to reassure them, introducing them to the community. We all felt their pain, like it was a common experience to us all. I felt that we had all been through some catastrophe; we had all helped one another to survive.

Arusha sat down next to me. The shaman and I exchanged glances. You just know things in dreams, and I knew that something important was happening. I was here experiencing this particular moment, because I was supposed to remember carefully.

If I could remember, then I could get to this safe place and avoid looking like the Holocaust arrivals across the table, or worse.

I knew what the shaman was thinking the same way I had seen through my unborn daughter's eyes.

"It's time for you to go," *Tatti said silently.*

I felt a little sad, thinking I would miss this place and all our friends.

"You have to go," *but he looked sympathetic.*

Go where?

"Back. To make the EcoVillage. To make this place you're in," *I heard him say.*

And it occurred to me that I knew exactly what he was talking about. It made perfect sense. I thought,

"Oh. Yeah, that's right. There's something I have to tell me, something Arusha has to tell me."

In dreams anything is possible, and it's like a computer file that gets unzipped over the course of time. You don't know what things mean to you in your present surroundings, but you do know what it means to you in the place you're at. I knew exactly what he was talking about.

FINDING THE FORCE 1:

What was stranger was that I knew exactly who everyone was. And we called it an EcoVillage.

I knew what it was for too, this place, just like you know what stuff in your house is for. I knew that we had been very careful about how we built it, what direction it faced, to get the most sunlight, that it was partly underground to retain heat in the winter, and coolness in summer. It was round, and very large, with emanating areas like spokes from the central area. There was food storage and preparation, housing, and some smaller meeting areas through different corridors. I knew there was a garden right outside, where flowers bloomed and vines draped over a huge patio where we liked to eat sit in spring and fall.

I also knew that we were self-sustaining, living from the land with everyone's help. We had begun to make our own clothes too, and some of us were wearing them. I know I felt sentimental about it, and the bright colored wool wrapped around my waist felt good.

We were calling him Tatti in the dream. I couldn't even remember his real name, and I was annoyed.

He started to move away and I followed him, leaving my family at the table. We walked back to another room together, to sit by a fire in a room full of strange paintings. I could see some of them in the firelight, but they were just out of my range of vision. There were silky tapestries hanging from the ceiling too, shifting with the rising heat from the fire.

Tatti drew my attention to him, and gave me instructions, clearly, in order.

- Develop your consciousness. Consciousness, or attention, both dreaming attention, and waking attention. This is your steering.
- Follow your heart. It is the place where you can be one with everything in Creation. This is your ship.
- Cultivate symbolic literacy. Allow your senses to receive symbolic meanings, from your life, and from your dreams. This is the language to read your map.
- Quiet your mind. Crystallize your intent in that silence, in that emptiness. This intent is the wind in your sails.

If you are here now, it means you can get back.
Then I was back outside, in the moonlit field of snow.

I saw a shiny black bird fly off, maybe a raven, with moonlight making different colors on its wings. For a moment, I was drawn back in. I could hear Arusha again, calling urgently.

"Don't forget the Poppies! Take the Poppies to the Shaman. He'll know what to do."

I saw the painting she was talking about. It had been on the wall.

A clay pitcher of surreal red poppies were sitting on a table. Perched on the edge of the table, a rainbow colored raven was drinking from the poppy pitcher, and a stairway led up, five steps, then six, to a darkened window with a crescent moon, and a star shining through.

Then it was gone, and I was in New York again.

I woke up from that dream knowing that something unusual had taken place, and that I had better follow the instructions given. I just knew, and I just did it. Nothing has ever seemed stranger and more normal all at once.

It was also easy to find the shaman, because I knew the first book I picked up, and the first page I opened to would have his picture. I opened my suitcase, pulled out the first book I felt. It was Mystery of the Crystal Skulls.

I opened it and there was his picture. Sure enough, it was the shaman from the dream.

I had to sit down; I felt sick because in an instant I had the knowing that something extremely outrageous was true. There was proof before my eyes. The man from the dream was staring right at me.

Patricio Dominguez.

Tatti

TIP 1: Develop Consciousness. Ways of doing that: Meditation, Yoga, Shamanism, Plant Medicine, Martial Arts

FINDING THE FORCE 1:

CHAPTER TWO

Roger Nelson: Princeton Global Consciousness Project (GCP)

Again the violet bows to the lily.
Again the rose is tearing off her gown.

The green ones have come from the other world,
Tipsy like the breeze up to some new foolishness.

      -Rumi

Princeton, NJ April 10, 2005

    Of all the material that I had spoken about with Patricio Dominguez, there were three questions that needed follow up:

1. What exactly, is consciousness, and could it extend to our entire planet? Could our planet be conscious of *us*? Should we be conscious of *her*? Are we all interconnected somehow?
2. Is there any evidence that something is happening leading up to 2012? Then what about Beyond 2012? If so, how does it work? What is happening as we approach this date? And after?
3. Can people actually live together in harmony in small, sustainable communities, like the one from my visions with Arusha? Could we improve our plight as humans, or are we just destined to be killer monkeys?

    Before asking questions about consciousness, though, we had better at least have a working definition.
    Merriam-Webster defines consciousness as:

1. **a:** the quality or state of being aware especially of something within oneself **b** : the state or fact of being conscious of an external object, state, or fact **c** : **AWARENESS**; especially: concern for some social or political cause
2. **2** : the state of being characterized by sensation, emotion, volition, and thought : **MIND**
3. **5** : the upper level of mental life of which the person is aware as contrasted with unconscious processes

So, consciousness means *being aware of one's perceptions, and mental processes, or mind, especially the "upper level"*. Could "upper level" refer to the place where we are all interconnected, or even tied into out planet's consciousness?

These were difficult questions, and I was happy to have experts to talk to.

According to the records of the masters, there are many paths that can lead to enlightenment. Yoga, Kung Fu, Shamanism, Buddhism, Zen, and many more, can all lead people into transcendental states where they glimpse what lies on the other side of our material robes. And they can even learn to manipulate the physical realm, based on the laws that come before the material world.

There is a form which lies underneath the robes of material reality, something that is accessible, and I believe the something that can take us there is consciousness, and it can connects us to the Eternal, the Divine.

Dominguez also spoke of people needing to realize that there are two parts to our nature, the divine and the mortal. The divine part is composed of a certain light, or "hue" and the other part is the carbon and water based biological mechanism, or "man". Together we are hu-man, more than just an animal, temporarily less than divine. He did say there are many paths to en-light-enment- or awareness of one's light aspect.

So I went and did a few months of research on that topic, to see if it would lead anywhere.

And, the answer seemed to correlate to the hu-man concept.

Apparently, once a disciple grasps that there is another, perennial, reality, the meanings of many teachings become clear. Once they see that there is a window that light comes through, they are often

FINDING THE FORCE 1:

are able to return repeatedly to an altered state of awareness. With disciplined meditation, it is possible.

With physical practice and diet in addition, it is probable.

With all that and the guidance of a master who has gone before, it is inevitable.

The student then becomes a bridge between the Material World and the various other Worlds, a connector between Earth and Heavens.

But the process of unlearning many of the things we are taught by society and our families takes time, and serious discipline. Many students give up their material life and seclude themselves. They fast, perform physical exercise, use specific meditation, ingest plant medicine, drum, journey…Austerity certainly characterizes the majority of them in some part, but there is also a rigid scientific organization behind most. The medicine formulas that have taken the masters to enlightenment seem to work if the student is ready. Then again, it seems there is also spontaneous enlightenment.

Before there was imperialism and dogma though, there were once many, many systems all over the world to lead the seeker to a different state of consciousness. That much I was able to ascertain for certain and has been proven beyond dispute (except to those who refuse to believe in anything "supernatural" at all).

Now that we know there is a way to achieve altered consciousness are we able to assume it can bring us closer to our Divine aspects? And what do people tend to take away from these experiences?

They seem to all come to the conclusion eventually that we are all interconnected by the part of us which is more Divine, or of more subtle essence. If we are all made up of the same Divine substance, we must all be connected.

Then there is the obvious. We all breathe the same air on this planet, live on the same carbon molecules, and drink of the same waters. We are more closely connected physically than anyone cares to admit. There is no such place as "away".

But are our minds connected?

What about a connection to our planet? Can we really expect to keep trashing everything and not be affected?

FINDING THE FORCE 1

When people talk about "Gaia" as a living being, then does this being have "consciousness"?

Years before I had conducted an interview with a really unique individual who might have some answers. I approached the familiar place in Princeton, nearby the campus of the University, where Roger Nelson had agreed to meet with me to talk about some of these things.

The first time I had met Roger Nelson was before he had "gone public" on major news with his work on consciousness, and his research at Princeton. I had been on assignment from an online publication called the Spirit of Ma'at, and he had granted me a lunch interview.

Since his project was the "Global Consciousness Project", it seemed likely he could shed some light on my questions.

The flowers were blooming that cold, wet, day as I made my way down the back roads of New Jersey with Adrian. We had an appointment at a Chinese restaurant. Though well into spring, the air was chilly and the drizzling mist everywhere, providing for a bone chill. Some hot Chinese soup would taste good.

Roger Nelson was a scientist researching the effects of mind and thought on the environment. He had worked for some time at the PEAR Lab (Princeton Engineering Anomalies Research), before branching off to do some similar, inventive work.

To understand the nature of what Roger tentatively called a discovery, it's important to understand the work of the PEAR Lab, which was established,

"...In 1979 by Robert G. Jahn, then Dean of the School of Engineering and Applied Science, to pursue rigorous scientific study of the interaction of human consciousness with sensitive physical devices, systems, and processes common to contemporary engineering practice."

In plain language, Jahn had a good job at Princeton, and didn't want to jeopardize it by doing paranormal research. He was interested in proving or disproving that humans could have an effect on machinery, though, so he found a way by studying something highly measurable.

FINDING THE FORCE 1:

If we have even a small effect on random events, then we could extend that hypothesis to the world around us too.

According to the book (*Margins of Reality*), which resulted from their work, Jahn (the Founder) and Dunne (who ended up running the lab) state:

"By virtue of the manner in which it exchanges information with its environment, orders that information, and interprets it, consciousness has the ability to bias probabilistic processes, and thereby to avail itself of certain margins of reality."

Thus, scientifically we can see, the mind does have a provable effect on the environment around us. This discovery means that at the outskirts of our physical realm, there is a margin where the mind does affect that ragged edge. Western science and Eastern/Native mystical traditions are both saying the same thing in this case.

Western science (to a certain point) says we're just here to observe, receive and process. And that may be true of our brain in some ways. Many mystical traditions say we create the experience around us with our minds, and are only limited by our limiting beliefs alone and together. There is a margin where it all comes together.

Our beliefs create a script for our life, the brain is like a holographic projector, and our lives can often become like a machine witnessing an unchangeable roller coaster ride.

But add in that slippery variable of mind and consciousness and things begin to change.

While Roger Nelson was working there the PEAR Lab proved that human intent has a measurable effect on reality, beyond what random chance could account for. They used machines that could register and calculate any deviation from the expected norm in situations where people were intending to influence machines. Turns out we can. Even machines are affected by our thoughts and intentions.

Though it doesn't seem that way to most of us, the gurus and shaman are right. Our thoughts and feelings and intentions shape the world around us, to one point or another. The degree to which we shape things consciously depends on our ability to be aware of both our unconscious (limiting beliefs) and our super-consciousness (collective and spiritual self).

So, Roger had originally worked on that project and then continued probing. If we have an effect on machines, what about on each other at a global level? Roger Nelson had created The Global Consciousness Project (GCP) in order to investigate the larger scope of our human effect on reality.

If a growing body of scientific evidence showed that "consciousness and intention have subtle but important effects in the world" as individuals, then did we all participate globally in some way, to shape our world?

Would it be possible to measure our effect together?

If so, how?

Roger ended up using a time-proven instrument from the PEAR Lab, which would monitor the levels of human static worldwide. Like an EEG that monitors consciousness through placing monitors on the head to detect brain waves, these devices are called EGG's. In the original interview I made:

Roger: *"We called them 'EGGs' after EEG – electroencephalograph, but we changed one letter to add Gaia – Electro Gaia Gram, or something like that. The devices are what we call random event generators, or sometimes, random number generators. It's not a program; it's a physical device that's creating something like the computer version of white noise."*

Me: *"So it's a fast coin toss with equal 50-50 odds each time?"*

Roger: *"That's about right. Every second, we gather 200 of these bits - it's like flipping two hundred coins. We count the bits, or how many heads you get when you flip two 200 coins.*

You would expect that answer to be around 100 each for heads and tails wouldn't you? Right? Plus or minus of course, the fluctuation that we refer to as standard deviation, which is about 7. The range of numbers we get is more like 70 to 130, though!"

So the events were randomly generated, precise, and unaltered physically. They were computers, simply providing a 50-50 event, and seeing if 50-50 is what really comes over the course of time. This graph

FINDING THE FORCE 1:

*shows visually the 1 in 50,000 probability that these numbers are **not** related to an event, or phenomena.*

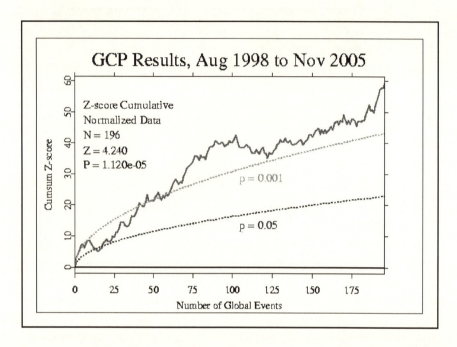

If the black line in that graph is what statistical probabilities would lead you to expect, you can see over time that the results get stranger and stranger. The movement away from the straight black line means that the evidence is farther each year from what would have been expected.

Certain events also showed striking deviation from the "norm." When all of our minds and feelings were together, such as during a tragic or emotional event, there were rather unusual variations from the normal expected data.

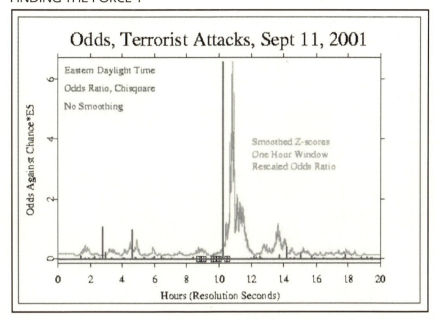

Even the untrained eye can see something going on in these graphs.

Roger's explanation is that when people's minds came together in the same direction over something, the effect was measurable, at least by his EGGs, and certainly also according to many people's experience over the centuries.

To quote from the GCP's website,

"We don't yet know how to explain the correlations between events of importance to humans and the GCP data, but they are quite clear. They suggest something akin to the image held in almost all cultures of a unity or oneness, an interconnection that is fundamental to life."

What does that mean to us all, individually?

In the original interview Roger's answer had been:

"We're like neurons in a way and the neurons don't know anything about the brain or consciousness, they just know what they need to know in order to get the job done. We should do the best we can to be good humans just like neurons do the best they can to be good neurons,

FINDING THE FORCE 1:
and the result will be a kind of interconnection that becomes comfortable at a greater level, at a deeper more profound level."

Now I was going to speak to him again, hoping to clarify how this all fit together with what the shaman had said.

When we arrived at the restaurant, Roger and I spent some time catching up and playing with the baby.

The food was a delicious treat, especially on a damp spring day, chatting about families and Roger's plans for upcoming trips to collaborate with other researchers around the world. He seemed really positive about how things were moving in the research community.

After lunch we walked around the area and saw the flowers blooming as baby pointed at everything and asked for sticks that he would periodically throw down. Roger spoke about an interview he had done recently for the CBS Nightly News in New York.

"So I finally decided to allow some media coverage of the project, and the reporter who showed up had really done his homework, so we were able to have a meaningful conversation about things. He asked really good questions."

"What was the best question he asked you?" I wanted to know what Roger considered a good question, since I was going about asking people questions herself.

"He pointed to the graph of the past seven years of data and recognized a severe downward trend, especially after 9-11. He got right to the point. He asked if it could be like some kind of planetary depression."

"And?"

"Well, I told him it's difficult to know, but that certainly was one interpretation of it."

"Is that your interpretation?" I asked.

"Things aren't looking too well out there are they? I mean they haven't gotten better as a result of the attacks, and the way people feel about the world around them certainly wouldn't be improving as a result either. Sure. It really could be a certain kind of malaise on a global scale. It would be hard to imagine that not existing."

FINDING THE FORCE 1

The three of us were walking through the fine mist and I had the baby covered in a wool serape from the recent trip to New Mexico. I felt the warmth of the baby and his closeness to my chest and really hoped that things weren't going to be getting any worse. A lot of this talk from Roger sounded just like the Maya Prophecies about the End of Times.

As we ended our walk, I looked down and saw a patch of daffodils, blowing in the breeze.

They looked like their centers were spinning. I got a nauseous feeling, and leaned on a tree for a moment.

The flowers were just like the ones in the Dream of the Flying Jaguar I had the night before. Reality was getting just a little too fluid lately. I suddenly remembered everything, and as I got into the car I began recording the dream series that begins this chapter.

TRIP 2: DREAM OF THE FLYING JAGUAR

There I was in a lush forest, thick and primordial, so moist and thriving, covered with every form of life. There were trees of every size and a blanket of thick hummus and vegetation on the floor of the forest. It was so thick that I could not walk. I was there with a handful of other people and I sensed they were also spiritual adventurers, and wished to explore.

Suddenly, I felt myself shift into a large cat's body, and when I leaped, I was able to fly through the forest through the trees, maybe fifteen feet up. From there I could see the entire forest, and could navigate, sailing through the canopy. Nobody else could follow though, and I eventually lost my dream mates.

I was the Flying Jaguar.
I could explore anything I liked.

Off in the distance, there was a cool looking pool. I wondered what it would feel like in a spirit body.

FINDING THE FORCE 1:

It felt good! There was very little difference between that and regular bathing. I could even take the waters into my mouth, and they were very refreshing. I had been thirsty from all the flying about!

Soon I was called to leave and explore options other than the eternally beautiful forest realms. To the West I could see there were cliffs of rock down below, with distinctive crevasses. Those dark jagged lines were really appealing. I came down to have a look.

As I approached through the air, bounding on the ground from time to time, the large cracks got closer, and almost sucked me in and up through them. Before I knew what happened, I was in a human body again, standing at the top of the cliff in a village.

There were many cozy little stores there, with glass windows full of shiny or delicious things. Any type of clothing, shimmering ornaments, extravagant foods, and furniture were displayed.

They were all very pretty, but it made me homesick for the forest. I wanted to be the Flying Jaguar again, and go home where I belonged.

But it was not so. I was forced to stay somehow, and tour the entire place, every building. I guess it reminded me of France, or New York City, wonderfully elegant and refined, with ribbons on all the little packages, and delicious smells.

There were restaurants where people were sitting talking, and they were talking about all their daily business. They were so completely wrapped up in their day to day affairs. They had no talk of the pulsing life beneath them in the forest. Like it didn't exist.

They were in theatres, watching films, while life was passing them by outside. The theatres were very dark, even at mid-afternoon, and people were actually smoking cigarettes inside, or something, it was thick with smoke so you could barely see.

In and out, in and out of all these stores they went. I could see women trying on clothes, children screaming for toys.

Groceries, little markets, dogs and birds and cats.

Then I was taken to the places where people were fornicating in dark seats in the top of a theater. I don't know why they were doing that there, but there were lots of them, and they didn't even notice each other. They just kept at it.

FINDING THE FORCE 1

None of them I saw outdoors in the streets even looked up to the sky once.

Not even the kids.

How could they all have totally forgotten about Nature?

When I tried to talk to them, they became annoyed, like I should just mind my own business, and leave them be.

They were very busy people, with long lists of things to do and goals to accomplish. If they were successful they would be allowed to eat in the nice restaurants and see movies and fornicate.

And they had been taught that those were the only things that existed.

But they were thirsty.

Or were they empty?

They were empty of that something that quenches the thirst all the way down to the bones. They were waiting for something more meaningful, but were too busy to pay much attention to that inner voice that calls us all.

That voice says to all of us,

Give me water to drink! I am thirsty! Nourish me so that I can grow! I am the spirit behind everything...See your interconnectedness with everything and you are part of me again!

After passing what seemed like several hours there, with no chance of interesting conversation or stimulus, I went back the edge of the cliff. I could see the pool of delicious waters glimmering below, and as I arrived, I saw bunches of daffodils blooming, waving in the breeze, looking right at me.

I was home again.

TIP 2: Consciousness Connects Us to a Larger Reality: What is our Relationship and how do we Communicate? Mind, Prayer, Practice.

FINDING THE FORCE 1:
CHAPTER THREE: John Major Jenkins

"The 2012 era is about the birth of something new on this planet, but it is also a death, the rupture of the womb-world that held us comfortably warm for millennia, unaware of the larger world outside of our limited sights."

-John Major Jenkins

Christian, Jew, Muslim, Shaman,
Zoroastrian, Stone,
ground, mountain, river,
each has a secret way of
being with the mystery,
each unique and not to be judged.

- Rumi

Orange County NY, 2005

Roger Nelson's work had confirmed that there is such a thing as planetary consciousness, and Dunne and Jahn's work proved that our thoughts and intent can affect reality. Nelson's project also showed the extension of that relationship to a planetary level. It showed that our consciousness as humans affects our planet, and we are all interconnected on some level.

My first question following up after Don Patricio Dominguez had been answered.

What about my second question?

Is there any evidence that something is happening leading up to 2012? If so, how does it work?

What is happening as we approach this date?

Having read a number of books on 2012, I felt that John Major Jenkins was a reliable source. Don Patricio had said that Jenkins was as good as a shaman (and better than some) in his interpretation of Maya Cosmology. Others said that he knew nothing and should leave Maya Calendrics to the Maya.

But in the absence of a Maya Shaman (and I had looked) I was left to the resources at my disposal.

Jenkins is the author of a number of books on the matter, (*Galactic Alignment, Maya Cosmogenesis 2012, Pyramid of Fire*) and they all essentially have to do with Maya Cosmology and the end of the Long Count on December 21 2012.

He lived with the Maya for some time, and understands some of their worldview and their shamanic rituals. Jenkins also pulls together diverse materials from Hindu, Egyptian, Hebrew and Maya cosmologies to paint a multi faceted picture of Earth Changes and Ancient Wisdom. He also includes some rich scientific documentation that seems to confirm the truth of ancient cosmologies.

I had written to Jenkins and he agreed to speak to me about his work. He also sent some CD's with excerpts of radio interviews. He spoke to me for some time initially and confirmed the basics. Later, further conversations would enrich and expand my initial understanding, and Jenkins was always generous with his time.

There was a lot of information in Jenkins' work, and it is somewhat difficult to boil it down to something that a modern human being living in our society in the US can understand. Our way of life is so completely foreign to these Primordial Traditions that we have long believed that they were backwards, or unevolved because they did not have the same way of life as us.

I mean, if they were so smart, then how come they didn't have cars, or even vehicles? Why did they just sit around staring at the night skies and dancing and celebrating life? How could they soar to such spiritual heights and profound understandings without microwave ovens? Hadn't they gotten it all backwards?

FINDING THE FORCE 1:

It seems that the Maya, as well as groups such as the Aborigines, the Kogi, to name a few, "flirted" with technological developments and then cast them aside as a dangerous and pointless exercise.

Because they saw themselves as part of the larger picture of the Universe and Creation, they sought to enhance their role and ability to delight in that. Their entire existence was based on their non-dualistic assumptions, which are not only beneficial spiritually, physically, and emotionally, but also scientifically accurate.

In the end they lived on this planet for millennia without creating mass extinctions and toxic waste, and used their bodies as their high technology. The profound understanding of the proper place of the human life form was the only development they saw necessary.

From that simple place it was possible for them to explore the Universe and Creation and to experience the profound beauty, complexity and elegance of Being. The development of Self Aware and Self Reflective Being is Creator's most supreme act.

This supreme act of creation itself was begun (at least in our local Milky Way Galaxy) in the Galactic Center. The Maya shaman-kings and astronomers watched carefully to understand and to express this beauty in their society. Their concern with calendrics was a manifestation of their desire to explore the vast realms of their Inner-Outer Universe, to commune with their Creator. By journeying ritualistically with the power of the mind, they touched God/Goddess/Creator in a real way, because life was begun with that light and that stardust at the Galactic Center.

They watched the skies because they knew what it has taken scientists centuries to 'discover' – that the movement of the stars and heavenly bodies is describing and determining the ongoing developments of Life itself:

FINDING THE FORCE 1

"In other words, the evolutionary heartbeat of humankind beats in rhythm with a higher, Galactic heartbeat, and it is our inner dialogue with our cosmic source that weaves the future...the human brain 'is modeled after the celestial vault and the human mind functions according to the stars, which are the ventricles and sensoria of the cosmic brain'" (Maya Cosmogenesis 2012).

While watching the night sky, the Maya documented the mechanics of the celestial clock, and they discovered that certain unusual but periodic alignments seemed to bring about certain parallel developments in our earthly reality. Their 20 Day Lords (day energies) and 13 numbers make an extremely accurate system for marking time and celestial events.

The 'Big One' for the Maya was the moment when the sun would rise into the dark path into the Galactic Center. The time leading up to this event which only occurs every 52,000 years (due to a wobble in our planet's orbit called precession) is supposed to be a time of transformation and preparation so that we can enter into a new phase of our human evolution.

Potentially there will be considerable disruption as these changes are taking place. This includes increased natural disasters, disturbances in society such as war and violence, and much more.

It ends up sounding a lot like what Don Patricio had said in the beginning. If we chose the wrong path, there would be no going back, and it was going to be a bumpy ride.

I was also concerned with finding any pieces of information that would demonstrate scientifically that this has happened in the past, and what kinds of events might have taken place. If there really are Cosmic tools for the transformation of humanity, then there should be some physical signs that this actually has happened before.

There are many books out now that demonstrate that this is in fact the case. "Fingerprints of the Gods" (Hancock) "The Day

FINDING THE FORCE 1:

the Sky Fell" (Flem-Ath) and the "Mysteries of the Great Cross at Hendaye" (Weidner/Bridges) are just a few.

The evidence demonstrates clearly that there have been major catastrophes periodically on our planet, and that our environment is a lot less stable than we generally believe. Not only are there periodic Ice Ages, but there are also periodic shifts in the magnetic pole, as well as what seems to be substantial shifts in the Earth's crust layer. Tropical plants have been found in what is now Siberia, and it seems they were taken there quickly, and froze en masse (Flem-Ath). The explanation for this is that perhaps the top layer of the Earth is sitting on a comparably solid magma layer that is sensitive to pressure, and can become liquefied under certain circumstances. This would allow the crust to rotate quickly, taking continents in the tropics to the Arctic region, practically overnight.

What's more, there are now ice core samples that date back many hundreds of thousands of years, which show periodic changes correlating roughly to these 52,000-year cycles. In Bridges and Weidner's work they found a scientist named Paul LaViolette who had been doing research that demonstrated a possible mechanism for these periodic changes.

LaViolette's research shows that there are periodic 'explosions' coming from the center of Spiral Galaxies, where the center shines brighter than all the stars combined. They were originally known as Seyfert Galaxies. Astronomers witnessed a "blinking" from Galactic Center of these spiral galaxies (like ours), and assumed it was an anomaly.

In fact, all spiral Galaxies do this from time to time, blinking on bright for hundreds and even thousands of years. When this happens, the blast first carries electromagnetic waves that move at close to the speed of light. This would have effects on communications and the electromagnetic fields of our bodies and the planet's system as well.

But there is a second wave of particles that is dust, and would eventually settle on the sun's surface, causing increased solar flare activity.

And it just so happens that right now our sun is going through one of those periods of very high flare activity. According to Mitch Battros of ECTV, NASA has issued a warning that our present cycle (Cycle 24) will be 50% stronger than the last one (23), which already brought about flares brighter than scientists even believed possible.

Don Patricio had mentioned that with these shifts, there was a substantial amount of energy coming in that would also cause a shift in people's consciousness. These high and intense energies would be the mechanism for the shifts occurring, and whoever could not come to integrate this level of consciousness would begin to "go haywire".

It seemed that all the time that this Maya just might hold water. What if the moment when the sun rises in December of 2012, this marks the general time frame of our solar system moving into a cloud of dust that will heat up our sun and cause shifts to occur in our evolution?

My second question had been answered, and all that was left was to have a conversation with Jenkins about it to confirm. The piece below is Jenkins' response to my questions.

Is there any evidence that something is happening leading up to 2012?

It certainly seems that something unprecedented is happening on the planet right now. Generally, the 20th century was unparalleled in terms of global wars, technological and medicinal breakthroughs, and, especially, massive development of

FINDING THE FORCE 1:

technologies. Of course, we've heard the old warning that every era thinks it is special, but, really, tangible evidence indicates quite clearly that the late 20th century is unparalleled. My suspicion is that, somehow, the galactic alignment is involved in this process.

How is present day life versus past life in Maya community?

On the level of average Mayan people, it hasn't changed much. However, the shaman-kings have been replaced by a foreign governing power. Encroachment of Western ways and values, and violent oppression and genocide, is a reality to the modern Maya. The classes of Mayan people that were involved, in ancient times, with "higher pursuits (math, astronomy, shamanism) has been compromised, but echoes still survive. The 260-day calendar survives unbroken today, but the Long Count calendar that gives us the 2012 end date has been lost for some 500 years. Elements of the Creation Mythology survive in the dance drama of Rabinal in Guatemala.

A basic perspective of Mayanism is what can be called non-dual consciousness, in which polar opposites are seen to NOT be mutually exclusive, as our own Western Cartesian philosophy would have us believe. Some ancient cultures, or let us say, metaphysical teachings, ascribed to a non-dual philosophy. Vedanta, for example. Basically, it is the "as above, so below" principle that is criticized by modern rationalists as superstitious. The processes occurring in the objective (outer) world reflect processes occurring in the subjective (inner) world. Said another way, spirit and matter are one from the non-dual perspective.

Was the Maya calendar "accurate"? Did their spiritual technology bring any benefits?

"Accuracy" of the calendar is a boring red herring. Yes, it was accurate. More importantly, it was comprehensive. The "calendar" embodies a philosophy of time and space that embraces many dimensions of human experiences, from biological to agricultural to spiritual unfolding and astronomical cycles.

Looking up into the sky on December 21 of 2012 we can see the visual portrayal of an important event in Maya Cosmology. The sun will rise into the Galactic Center's "dark rift". This dark rift is considered to be the birth canal of the Great Mother, and when the sun rises into it, this marks the fertilization of the Great Mother. A New Time will be born then, a time, presumably, of higher consciousness, and an awareness of our connection to the Universe?

...I like to think of 2012 as the CENTER of Mayan time, not a new time, strictly speaking. New, perhaps, in the sense that we've been alienated from being connected to the cosmic source. But it's really about remembering our true natures – returning to a centered place.

Is there any scientific evidence that something akin to the Maya predictions is happening on our planet right now?

All of this is explored in Galactic Alignment. This area comprises the second part of the work, that of speculating on empirical models by which the galactic alignment might affect consciousness and/or earth changes. I strongly encourage readers to not confuse the as yet ambiguous evidence in this domain for

FINDING THE FORCE 1:

evidence that the Maya were or were not aware of the galactic alignment and intended their 2012 date to target it.

My reconstruction of the galactic alignment's presence in ancient Maya thought is much more cogent than the possible models for the galactic alignment's efficacy. At this early stage in the investigation of this area, we cannot say much for certain. It's not really my department. However, I chastise the supposed PhD-holding physicists who are appropriating my alignment work to write books on apocalypse and doomsday. They supposedly provide "evidence" that the world will be destroyed because of the galactic alignment, but in fact they are irresponsible, opportunistic idiots.

What is happening as we approach 2012? Could it be that there are magnetic shifts taking place because of the fields emanated from the Cosmic Center?

Yes, maybe.

What kind of effect would it have on our planet? Is it possible, as some indicate that we may experience the greatest mass extinction in 65 million years?

It appears to be crises of re-connection with our true selves. We are experiencing the greatest mass extinction in 65 million years – because of humanity's greed and avarice that has arisen by our angst from being dissociated from our true selves. (Species are disappearing by the minute)

What kinds of attitudes and shifts would tend to help us ride these waves of shifting energies?

FINDING THE FORCE 1

Do the age-old perennial work of sacrificing your illusions, putting the ego back into right relationship with the eternal divine self. Initiate yourself into the grand perennial vision of wholeness, healing, and unity. You know how to do it.

Is it possible that a daughter in a happy future could contact a mother to guide her along a pathway of safety through these times?

Yes. Future time might also refer to higher consciousness.

Why do you think the Maya didn't' develop certain technologies? Could they foresee the negative consequences? Is there something good about living as a community and doing things by hand?

My work, as published in Maya Cosmogenesis 2012 has been to reconstruct ancient Mayan cosmology, to sift through millennia of eroding ideas, sorting through layers of garbage, to emerge with an understanding of what the ancient Maya considered to be important. For the most part they didn't care about wheels, calendar gears as envisioned by modern scholars, or anything close to a material technology.

But they were clairvoyant engineers of time travel and architects of hyper-dimensional wormholes in space-time. They were masters of the structure of the universe and they were astronomer-mathematicians who could perceive and calculate the timetables of human unfolding. All this without ironworks, telescopes, microwave ovens, light bulbs, or re-sealable plastic bags. The greatest achievement of the Maya, and the greatest knowledge their living representatives can offer us today, is in the field of spiritual technology, so that we can develop or rediscover our full human potential. ("Ancient Spiritual Technologies": Published in Psychic Reader, Berkeley, California, August 2001.)

FINDING THE FORCE 1:

This perspective seemed a lot more positive than things had at the outset, with the doom and gloom predicted by the Hopi Stone and Don Patricio. It even seemed a bit brighter than Roger Nelson's graphs of Gaia's depression.

I was starting to feel better all the time, and wondering if perhaps my own shifting perspective might not also be shifting the world around me somehow. I had come a long way from the beginning of terrifying visions and desperation. In fact, I even started to get some sleep too.

It's important to also mention that Roger Nelson did eventually read the chapter and said he was somewhat saddened by how negative his work seemed. He said that he is an eternal optimist, and that he should like people to know that, and also feel this too. Here is what he said in his e-mail:

"The main thing is that I find there is compelling scientific evidence for the interconnectedness of people with each other and with the world. It is subtle but real, and it is really important. There are qualities that are part of this picture that need to be understood by more of us.

Some, the poets and the spiritually practiced know, and more of us half-know about the deep beauty, know, for example, the meaning of compassion and love. Babies and mothers know that Spring unfolds a crystalline beauty each year, and that our intention and expectation make the colors richer and more intense.

Humans have the ability to learn this; we just need encouragement to let magic live."

TRIP 3: DREAM OF THE ESCAPE OF THE TRIBE

The armed guards are escorting us down into the depths of a huge ship. There are four of us in total, lined up, and the guards are not going to harm us, it seems, but they are serious about the mission of taking us to our quarters on the lower levels of the ship.

The ship is huge, like a Princess Royal Cruise Liner the size of a city, with towers, hundreds of decks, plants growing from the sides, and millions of tiny round cabin windows. There are even decks where I could see people outside sunning, looking at the sky.

As we are marched into the belly of the boat, I can see wonderful little restaurants with different themes.

The Spanish restaurant has little tables that look just like the tables I remember in Barcelona, and there are menus of delicious food. I want to stop and eat something, but it's just not on the list of things to do for our escort.

Elevators and stairs and great open interiors with chandeliers, music, huge TV screens, disco balls, and every kind of amusement are available. But I don't see any human beings other than the ones working at the service areas. No one is enjoying all these wonderful playgrounds at the moment.

We march quietly down to our allotted room.

I ask why I am going to the basement. Couldn't I have one of those nice rooms above with the deck and plants and all?

"Stop making trouble. You and all your ideas. Maybe when you learn to do as you are supposed to you will get a promotion," *says the guard in back.*

But I was just trying to help.

"Rabble Rouser," *says the guard in front of me through the side of his mouth.*

Well, OK then.

Guilty as charged.

When I grow up I want to be an itinerant shaman.

Way down somewhere below, in what looks like it may be the staff quarters, we arrive at our cabin.

There is no violence in the way they are doing things, as they lead us around winding stair ways.

Just some disdain and the threat of abuse.

FINDING THE FORCE 1:

We are told to enter, and that we should stay quiet and go to sleep for a while. I see that there are four single beds lined up from the cabin window to the door.

The guards leave, the door closes, and like a little kid I start looking through the drawers.

The others look at me and raise their eyebrows a bit, kind of shake their heads, and go ahead to lying down as they were instructed.

Looking through the drawers I find some dark jeans, Doc Martins, and a white v-necked t-shirt. I have a backpack like the one I always carry.

Before too long I notice that the window is like that of many basements. It leads right out to freedom! Though the window is high up, I know we can climb out and make our way by dropping into the water.

"Let's go!" I cry, and they all sit there looking at me from their beds. They look at me like I'm nuts, and shake their heads no.

Naturally, that doesn't stop me.

I climb out through the window, and land on the grassy ground in front of a lovely beach. I can see right there in the harbor is a little boat with oars. Palm trees, balmy breeze, and the works.

I stand there and look, and I just can't see any reason why people would stay inside the ship. What is everyone doing in there? From the shoreline down by the little yellow boat, I look back and see lights on in millions of tiny round windows. The ship is massive, and looks to be quite full.

Still, I can't get it, because I feel I have an important mission to fulfill, one that no one else can accomplish. I sling the backpack into the boat and begin to row down to the next bay over.

The magical colors of dusk light the sea as the sun lowers to the horizon, and the tiny crescent moon shows a thumbnail above. Rowing happily, I am free, and I know that I will find my destiny.

I call out a happy song as I go, and in the next bay I see a motorized boat. I hop into that one and set off for a longer journey, watching the stars come out bright all around. The sunset is a delicious gold and coral, and it has the epic feeling of adventure.

FINDING THE FORCE 1

Before long I come to the next bay, and there are flowers everywhere, and lush green vegetation. I notice there is a vehicle parked on the road in front of the beach,

It's a sparkling sky blue, one of those vintage cars, like a Cadillac, with fins and shining chrome. I can see there are people in there waiting for me. My brothers and sisters!

Its lights go on and off as the driver hears my arrival!

I cut the motor and cruise in to shore, pulling the boat onto the sand, throwing the anchor over into the bay.

"Hey guys! What a relief," I say as I approach the car. *I knew who it was in the vintage Caddy.*

The interior is a creamy white leather, very soft. The driver nods his head and I see a bunch of dreadlocks moving about as he says,

"Fasten up. Let's go."

The last colors of the sunset are fading as we head into that direction. I see his hands on the white leather steering wheel are an opalescent brown. The other members of the car are seated on either side of me in back, they are younger little ones, hair tied back and eyes gleaming.

There is something unusual about their eyes. They are big and round and very dark. They are so cute!

I notice the hands on the steering wheel don't look quite normal. You can almost see through them.

When I look down, it is the same with mine. They glow like a light brown Mother of Pearl.

And then the skies peel apart in a weird pattern and the setting sun opens its mouth like a portal springing out of the inside of a flower. The green tendrils in the middle are a superhighway through space time, like a wormhole. And the Caddy isn't exactly a car.

A few seconds later, we are gone.

I am going Home.

FINDING THE FORCE 1:

TIP 3: Ancient Civilizations had Advanced Technology in Time Keeping and Non-Dual Cosmology. Energies Shift Over Long Periods of time.

CHAPTER FOUR

Joseph Chilton Pearce

The breeze at dawn has secrets to tell you;
Don't go back to sleep.
You must ask for what you really want;
Don't go back to sleep.
         -Rumi

Rhinebeck New York, April 2005

  Joseph Chilton Pearce has been railing against the ills of modern society since before I was born, in 1974. In fact, he had already written an international best-selling book called *Magical Child,* which should have changed the way people see child rearing and our entire existence.
  From the looks of things out there, it didn't. In fact, I wonder who bought and read it. If it was a best seller, I guess none of the millions of people who read it really took it seriously. That was not a problem for me. I took it very seriously.
  I took it to heart so much that it really disturbed me. I read it shortly after I gave birth, usually as I was feeding the baby in our rocking chair, and it about gave me a nervous breakdown. I am not kidding when

FINDING THE FORCE 1

I say it was all I thought about, and all I cared about, trying to get things right for my child, so he could reach his full potential, and so I wouldn't end up scarring him for life and destroying his neurology.

Finally I realized that there was no way a single person in modern society could possibly achieve what Pearce claims is required in order for us to reach our full potential as human beings. Then I got really angry.

Let me explain.

Our potential as human beings is to be able to interface with our planet and with our surroundings in a harmonious fashion and to live in a state of bliss with Nature, and the Universe. We should be able to bend reality to one degree or another, in ways such as fire walking, precognition, telepathy and so on. No big deal. Modern research has proven all this to be completely possible. Most of us just don't ask ourselves why it's not happening then. Well, that's not Pearce's problem. He asks that question, and a lot more.

Pearce explains (in many different books, in many different ways) that we are not, in fact, separate from our surroundings. Though we believe ourselves to be witnessing a reality around us, and to be on a riverboat ride watching things go by, in fact, the truth is that we are the boat, the river, and the creators of the show. We are not actually separate from the world that surrounds us, and we are able to influence and affect our reality.

It is our belief that we are Separate that causes our capacities to become dormant, and to cut us off from our birthright, to live In the Garden, and as caretakers of our planet. We should also be free to roam the Universe and to experience various different levels of reality, and different dimensions at once.

And hooray, modern science proves all this. We now know for fact that Metaphysics from around the world is all fairly accurate.

All of the Ancient Peoples that Imperialism has enslaved and destroyed were "right" and our own technology and modern society, bought with blood, has come full circle to where we have "discovered" that the Indigenous/Aboriginal/Ancient Peoples of the world were quite correct.

FINDING THE FORCE 1:

We are one with our surroundings. We can and do interface with plant and animal life all around us, and we can mold our reality and live in a state of peace with our environment. We can live joyfully, and we were meant to. The nuts and bolts of it are fairly simple, when explained properly.

Matter is created as the result of fields. Fields are geometric shapes where the lines are areas of increased probability of finding subatomic particles called electrons. Electrons are the particles that orbit around the nucleus of an atom, and the number of these electrons essentially determines what substance that atom will be.

But electrons are pretty slippery when it comes right down to it. It's hard to know much about an electron. The more you know about one thing, the less you know about another, and so the observer affects the electron by observation. They also pop in and out of the space-time continuum, and exhibit some really funky abilities that indicate that time and reality are extremely fluid on that subatomic level.

Pearce describes an aspect of electron behaviors as "shopping" for possible realities. He uses the analogy of a couple going to look at every house on a certain block before they decide which one to move into.

Electrons visit many different possible realities before they 'settle' on one so to speak, and come into physical reality. When they do come into physical reality, it is because they have resonated with something in the creator of that reality – you or me.

Resonance means that they have something in common, and that they can 'go together'. The commonest analogy is that of a musical note being played in the same room as a stringed instrument, such as a piano. Striking a C note on another instrument in that room will cause the C string on the piano to vibrate, because they share the same wave shape that creates that note. The same holds true with fields.

Something in our minds is the attractor for manifestation, for solid items before us. Pearce describes over and over in each book how our brain is not a sensory device so much as it is a projector. He says that we confuse things. If you are watching a slide presentation projected onto a screen, then you realize that there is a projector. Well,

FINDING THE FORCE 1

our brain is the projector of our experience, a highly complex series of fields that are created by our brain cells connections.

The connections are made by neurons, tiny little string like cells that all establish relationships. The neurons gather information and make a map of the terrain of life, by association, like a filing cabinet. Experiences are sorted by commonalities and a file is opened for each new experience, and its relationship to other experiences is stored, and this eventually creates networks that give rise to 'meaning' in our experiences. There are significant shifts in our organization of those networks at birth, age 1, 7, 11 and 15. Eventually we start functioning from the map we have compiled of the terrain, rather than in the terrain itself. Somewhere in there we lose our ability to function properly and reach the pinnacle of human capacity. If any stage is not completed properly, then we are left with disconnection, Separation from The Garden, or Nature.

Pearce's latest adds also that the heart is the key to unlocking our potential. The heart is more than a muscle to pump blood.

It's a fourth brain comprised mainly of the same material (neurons) as the brains in our skull, and also secretes the hormones that create our emotional experience. When acting in harmony, the heart is capable of emitting a rather large field, and comes into unison with our other three brains, and then runs our experience here. These electromagnetic fields made by the heart are measurable and presumably are what run our experience.

However, with all of the mind-chatter that we have running in our brains– which is caused by stress, anxiety and chronic depression of all sorts – the heart cannot function as it should. Mind-chatter is that running dialogue of thoughts, words, desires, plans, worries etc. that meditation and all kinds of spiritual practice is supposed to help eliminate.

The reason why that mind-chatter cripples our ability to function, and shuts down the heart is because, though the heart does run our experience through its hormonal secretions, it simply takes orders from our brain. It cannot reason, cannot qualify the information being sent to it.

FINDING THE FORCE 1:

So, if I am running around worrying about money and not having enough, then I actually *experience* that feeling of not having enough. The heart just takes orders from the brain saying whatever its saying, whether we know that that tape is running or not.

Maybe your brain has a recording of "It's not enough...Worry worry worry I suck, life sucks I don't know how I'm going to make it...I'll never get that raise, I have to make more money, my partner doesn't love me, the kids are a mess...etc." Everyone has their tape recordings of mind-chatter, and they come from our very experiences in life.

As that tape runs, it is sending orders to the heart, which is creating that emotional state. As one *feels* that experience, commanded from the brain, created hormonally by the heart, then one attracts the events that will play that out in reality. Those electrons that are house shopping before manifesting are looking to find something they resonate with, that strikes the same chord.

So that's why when it rains it pours. If you are feeling down, those electrons are going to move into the crappiest house on the block, and manifest what the heart is emitting, as instructed by the brain chatter, without beings able to qualify it.

Stuck in a world rife with violence and materialism, the brain chatters away, sending messages of alarm and terror to the heart, which then produces that for us over and over.

Pearce claims that a spiritual practice is the only escape from that cycle. Actually, spiritual practice was designed to quiet mind-chatter and helps us to resonate with new possibilities and expand our awareness of our co-creation of reality so that we can begin to raise our consciousness in our reality.

The problem is that our society cripples us at every turn of the bend; from our birthing practices to daycare and on to every aspect of childrearing we practice, including our education system and television as the head enemies of our delicate but powerful neurology that manifests our world.

It's all a slippery slope geared towards reproducing human beings who are so stressed out that they never have a chance to ask themselves if a different existence is possible, let alone how to achieve a different existence.

For example, Pearce claims that even saying "no" to a child is devastating. I guess that means my kids are S.O.L. (Hooray for yoga.)

Seriously though, he says it's our job as parents is to provide an environment where: 1) Strong bonding between mother and child takes place beginning in utero, 2) A natural birth takes place in a quiet and stress free environment, 3) The mother is constantly present for the first year, 4) We do not use that bad word "no" because it makes our children feel "unloved" and 5) No educational material is introduced before the appropriate time because it forces the child to sacrifice the appropriate development necessary at that age (reading and reasoning are saved for beyond age 7 or 11).

It's a tall order, and it's what leads to the need for a different approach if these instructions are taken seriously.

Now you can see why reading his books can really cause a lot of stress for the parent who is wondering how they're going to run a home. I constantly had these worries nagging at me about how I was ruining Adrian's chance at healthy neurology and full potential. Meanwhile my child was running my home, and that wasn't a happy prospect for him at the ripe age of 12 months!

In the end, I was very angry with the people who suggested that a home without discipline and a baby breastfeeding all night was the way to provide a good environment. I was certainly over the edge of nervous exhaustion, was mentally fatigued and my child was miserable because he couldn't figure out why Mommy and Daddy were so unhappy.

With a demanding speaking schedule and a new book on the way, a best-selling author is hard to get an audience with. As I have mentioned, I just barely have enough journalistic credentials to say honestly that I am requesting an interview as background research for a novel.

I had to dig up Pearce's number by surfing the thread of synchronicity. 'Synch surfing' works like this:

First you decide what you want, and set your intent. It's best to clear and quiet the mind, and then say it out loud, or write it down.

FINDING THE FORCE 1:

Next you pay careful attention to what you feel called to do, and you simply do it. That may mean picking up the phone, walking out the door or standing on your head.

In this case, I was convinced that someone I knew had his phone number, and began calling some friends who were into home schooling. It turned out that one of them had a number for a woman who had just had Pearce as a speaker at a school up in Massachusetts, and she provided me with his number.

I forced myself to simply call him, and ask him for an interview. He was coming to a speaking event nearby at the Omega Institute, and so I offered to pick him up from Albany airport.

"This is Joe Pearce," he answered. I was confused, because it hadn't occurred to me that he would call himself that.

Really famous individuals somehow shouldn't answer their own phone, and even less address them self so informally. Where was all the pomp and circumstance?

After very little conversation, and just a few questions about the topic of the novel he agreed to allow me to pick him up. When I asked him why he would agree to let a complete stranger pick him up from the airport, he said you just have to have a little faith in life sometimes. I hoped I wouldn't disappoint him.

Even better, Omega Institute was kind enough to put me and my family up for the weekend, and grant access to a number of speakers from their *What the Bleep* conference.

Fred Alan Wolfe, Masaru Emoto and Jose and Miguel Ruiz would all be there that weekend presenting on related topics, and Omega granted me entrance to all of their presentations, very generously. I felt like a child, excited and nervous, with access to all the answers to the big questions about life. The novel seemed to be shaping up, and the Universe had granted my wishes.

Perhaps intent did work after all.

Seek and ye shall receive?

When Pearce walked up the runway from the arriving flights, I was very surprised. He was really quite a bit different in person than I

FINDING THE FORCE 1

expected. In fact, he looked exactly like he had in the dream, and nothing at all like his pictures.

He was wearing a trench coat, hat and shiny leather shoes. He was looking very stylish, I have to add, especially when you take into consideration that he is at least 85 years old. And if his looks don't impress you, all he has to do is open his mouth. He's sharper than you could imagine – unless you have read his books that is. Then you realize what's behind them.

He jumped into my little car, and I pulled out the directions for Omega Institute. He looked concerned.

"You've never been there before?"

"No, I haven't," I said looking at him. "But I do have good directions and a map, and you."

"Well, I thought you had been there a number of times. Are you sure you're going to be able to get there?"

"I think we'll be fine."

He reached into his carrying bag and pulled out some food.

"Mind if I have a banana and some milk?"

"No, not at all."

"It's the best thing you can eat for yourself. I have to keep myself in shape you know. You can go ahead with the interview."

I hadn't really expected to have to conduct the actual interview in the car while driving on a busy highway. My recorder wasn't going to sit very nicely bumping along the highway. And he had no pockets.

"I was hoping you would have some time once we got there," I said, looking worried.

"We'll see about that when we get there. Let's just get started," and Pearce looked worried too.

"OK. Can we just chat a little first and see where things head?" I suggested.

"Sure. That'll be fine, he sighed, shaking his head as he chewed on his banana."

There was no way I was going to delve into an interview with him at that point, and I thought I would pick his brain for answers to the basic problems we face as parents. The reader probably has some idea already about the burning issues on my mind at the time.

FINDING THE FORCE 1:

"Look," I started, "I have an infant who is a pretty unusual child to start off with, and let's say he's very driven. I'm not getting much sleep at night because he won't rest, and then by day he's making me crazy. He won't listen to me and he's into everything. I can't get any rest, day or night.

According to you, I am not supposed to say "no" to my child. What am I supposed to do?"

"Your job as a parent is to create an environment where you do not have to say no to your child." Pearce still looked worried. Probably he had noticed by this point that I had big bags under my eyes, and that I was pretty tense. In fact, the truth was I was quite angry. He was probably starting to wonder if I was a terrorist or something.

"But how am I supposed to do that? I can't put everything out of reach and I can't get any sleep and I can't figure any of this out and I have no one to help and he's one of those Crystalline Kids and I am having some really strange visions that he brought with him and my husband doesn't sleep either and all the baby has ever done is scream and I can't let him run my home and I just don't know what to do anymore."

Pearce was done with his milk and banana and was starting to fumble nervously with the directions. He looked up at me and repeated what he had said before:

"It's your job as a parent to make sure that you don't have to say no. You have to figure that out.

"But he's one of those Crystalline kids they are talking about. You know, the successor to the Indigos. I must be one of those or something, because my life has been pretty strange, but this kid is really a trip. I just can't keep up with him. He's supercharged, and it seems as if he can read my mind."

"He can. For the first year at least. Mother and child are simply one.

As far as the Crystalline kids go, I really didn't put much stock into it, but I do have some friends out in California who have been working with them, and apparently there's something to it. I even saw one once in the airport."

"How can you tell?" I was wondering if the description would match up with my son's.

FINDING THE FORCE 1

"Well, you'll see an extended frontal lobe, very bright, piercing eyes, and often times some other unusual characteristics. The one I saw in the airport looked right at me like he knew exactly who I was. He wanted me to walk over, so I did. He was with his mother and grandmother, and the mother wasn't all that happy about me coming over. Very, well, you could almost say domineering, very strong willed.

Most of all it seems that these children are coming to mothers who are completely independent and strong willed. Women who determine their own destiny, call their own shots, and usually stay at home mothers. They are here to accomplish something, and they will use their situation of birth as a springboard for that. They have chosen carefully. Are they telepathic? Are they super humans? I don't really know, but I don't think so. Or I didn't."

I remember thinking it was very interesting that Adrian had chosen me, but was grinding me into the dirt. It would be a long time before I got a handle on him, and it would be a long uphill battle, requiring all of my strength and confidence as a mother.

At the time though, I was really in bad shape, and a 1-year old baby was running my household, and running my husband out of job after job because no one in the house could sleep.

So, though I was happy to hear the confirmation that indeed something unusual was happening, I was still concerned about how in the world I was going to handle my son. He was now not only was keeping me up all night, but was driving me into the ground by day, fast fast fast.

"All right then, he's definitely one of those. So how am I supposed to deal with my son? I'm not supposed to say no to him during the day, and he's running me ragged. I'm not supposed to night wean him, or also I run the risk of destroying his neurology. But how am I supposed to live? Cook? Clean? Eat?? My husband can't hold down a job like this!"

I was getting hysterical, because this man wrote the only information I had ever found about children that made any sense at all, and I thought he would have some answers.

"Look, the most important thing is that he feels loved unconditionally, Crystalline or no.

FINDING THE FORCE 1:

I think we better change the subject now and move on," said Pearce, even more worried.

"You're right, OK." I nodded.

"I read your manuscript on my way here. I have to say, I don't usually like science fiction, but I did enjoy it. Especially your description of the community."

I was really happy he had read the chapters. But he had missed the point.

"It's not science fiction," I told him, looking at him to see if he was serious.

"What do you mean?" he replied.

"It's really happening, somewhere, someplace. I don't have a daughter, but apparently I do. Her name is Arusha and she is very clear about everything. She is guiding me around this community where we are all living. It's an eco-spiritual community based on the Tree of Life, she says. And from what I've seen, it makes sense."

"Hmm. I didn't know that. That makes it even more interesting."

I was wondering if he was just playing cat and mouse with me. He did continue though.

"You might want to get in touch with this friend of mine – Charles Eisenstein. He's on a similar track, concerned about where humanity is heading, and how we can return to a better way of life. You can read his book online, though I told him he shouldn't put it up there for free."

"What's his name?" I asked.

"Eisenstein. Like Einstein, almost. *The Ascent of Humanity* is the name of his book. You can find it right there online.
He was a yoga teacher at first, and has become a popular professor, speaking about the same type of material that you are addressing, especially if this is real."

"It is real, and my son brought it with him, and he just won't let it go until I have taken care of it."

"Do you know where you are going?" Pearce asked again, worried.

"Sure I do. I have directions."

"But you've never been there?"

"No, I haven't," I replied.

"I thought you had been there before. We should stop and ask for directions."

"I think we'll be fine. These MapQuest directions usually work out very well."

"Well, I'm pretty sure you just missed the turn back there for Omega. It looked familiar," Pearce insisted.

Joe Pearce was becoming more and more uneasy, perhaps about getting lost, about my concerns, about the whole conversation. I was really relieved in the end when got there without much trouble, and my family was waiting at the reception area.

Pearce got out of the car and looked across the way to where Adrian was hanging from Aaron's chest in the baby carrier and asked,

"Is that your son?"

"Yes. "

"Oh he's definitely one of them. Looking at him. He's looking at me from all the way over there, locking eyes. Wow. I haven't seen one of these guys since the airport and that woman. And I didn't get to interact with him because she wouldn't let me anywhere near. "

He walked over and met Aaron and Adrian and shortly thereafter was whisked away by the staff.

I never got my interview, but I did get to see him speak the next day. Apparently the material I was inquiring about was really old news. Before the red carpet was rolled out, I asked him,

"What are you speaking on tomorrow?"

"The only thing I ever speak on anymore. The Heart-Mind connection."

With that the little figure strolled away.

TRIP 4: DREAM OF THE MELTING METROPOLIS
Orange County, New York, April 2005

It wasn't enough to have strange visions and dreams of an unborn daughter in a world in some impossibly beautiful future.

FINDING THE FORCE 1:

Sometimes the dreams turned dark and became nightmares. I felt like I had prayed for something so vastly different than the life I was leading, that pieces of me were just being ripped to shreds and rewoven so as to create a different pattern. Some things just had to go, get pulled at, cut out, retied, and repaired with different threads. The Universe was refashioning my destiny as I had prayed, but it wasn't the easy ride I had thought.

We should be careful what we pray for, you know. When you are on the way to getting it, sometimes it doesn't feel as good as you thought it might. And the more you cling to what you

Just after my meeting with Roger I had a series of terrible dreams, and one in particular lead me to my next interview.

See, I didn't know who I was going to speak to next, I just knew that things were beginning to take the shape of something, and I had to put the pieces together just right.

In this dream, I was driving madly around the center of the largest city I have ever seen, trying to escape the impending disaster all around me.

There were really no people left, except for my son, and me. We were doing our best to maintain our calm, and feeling eerily centered in the surreality. Cars abandoned on the sides of the streets were sinking into the ground as the earth trembled and thickly paved streets buckled like sandpaper.

It seemed that the sky was falling and the earth was rising from its center all at once. I couldn't orient myself because I couldn't see the sun for all the buildings above our heads.

Skyscrapers blotted out the blue sky but for small pieces. Flows of lava poured from the cracks in the earth, and smoke rose in wisps where the broad fingers of bright lava devoured things. The lava glowed bright orange in the oddest way, since even in broad daylight it was dark in the shadow of those monstrous buildings.

For a while I was still driving, and then I came to a place where I had no choice, and was stuck in the center of two lava flows. As they devoured my car's wheels, I opened the door, and grabbed the baby. I put him into the baby carrier and he was strapped in tight to my chest, facing outwards. I had only one path that could lead me to safety, albeit temporary. But it seemed better than the fate that my car wheels had just met, sizzling and disappearing slowly into the orange blobs.

I was being forced to enter a tower that was being eaten by the lava, bit by bit.

Running into the building, I noticed that the baby wasn't crying - For once, Adrian wasn't crying! In fact, he was laughing.

That's funny! He thinks this is funny. He's totally amused, for once. Oh, that's because this is a dream. It's always the funniest things that make you wake up into a dream!

I ran and ran up and up and up the stairs of a huge skyscraper whose multiple staircases were bigger than a house itself. As I ran up the stairs I could feel the floors settling into the lava flow now surrounding the building, absorbing it.

"Thump!"

*When a floor was devoured, the building would make a huge "Thump!" and then moan once more. It was like a creepy rhythm section. With the addition of the shattering glass, the effect was complete. A symphony of destruction and Gaia Herself was the conductress. Mother Nature was reclaiming her own materials and just saying **no** to what we had done with her parts.*

And the baby kept on cooing. I had never heard him make that sound before.

Eventually I found myself in an even stranger situation, at the top of all those massive stairs. I arrived at a penthouse cabaret disco bar with panoramic windows...A front row view of the impending disaster, from the top of a building sinking slowly into the depths of molten iron, a burnt offering.

And there I was at the top of this building at a cocktail bar. It was very dark inside and I knew everyone. All the lawyers I had ever known were sitting around having martinis. To top it off, Frank Sinatra and Dean Martin played in the background through large speakers, and the disco ball sparkled all around the room, making little droplet specks.

The bartender was telling a joke as I walked up to try to get someone's attention:

"Whaddya call a bar full of lawyers at the bottom of a lava flow?"

FINDING THE FORCE 1:

A good start!

And everybody roared.

So everyone was drunk, and just sitting around telling bad jokes. I kept pointing out the windows and they laughed harder as they watched me.

I started laughing too, because I realized the baby was waving his arms around madly and gurgling, apparently making light of what Mommy was doing, mimicking every move with those tiny little hands. I must have looked like a complete joke, even if anyone had been sober enough to listen.

Everyone was telling jokes as the building moaned and sunk into the ground, tilting and jerking a bit from time to time. The building's percussion section thumped in time to Frank and Dino. You could see we were sinking lower and lower looking out the windows, and they were all just laughing and drinking their martinis.

Some of them were pissed they didn't have enough cigarettes, because after all, who was worried about lung cancer anymore?

Save yourselves! Hello! Isn't anyone paying attention?

But then, why wasn't I saving myself?

Because there was nowhere to go.

A couple of Scottish guys were telling stories over in the corner, and I thought I might be able to get through to them. At least they weren't lawyers.

They just wanted to tell me a story. I had finally given up and as they handed me a pint of some green liquid, they told their stories.

"So we were just in Rome you know," says Guy 1.

"Yeah we went to the Vatican and saw the Pope," Guy 2.

"Well, we were so inspired that we thought we'd go have dinner and toast to him."

"How did that go?" I asked, sipping the green liquid.

Scottish Guy 1: We ended up pukin' our guts out in the middle of the street. It was so bad we could see what we had eaten for dinner.

Guy 2: Yeah, it was a real chop carrot job.

Me: So what made you throw up?

FINDING THE FORCE 1

Guy 1: Well we asked the bartender what the Pope likes to drink and he said Crème de Menthe.

Guy 2: So we said 'Alright, give us a pint of that then.'

Guy 1: No wonder they carry the guy around in a litter.

I realized I was in the middle of a dream as I took a sip of what was in my pint glass. Crème de Menthe. Nobody drinks pint glasses of Crème de Menthe, and plus that was a really old joke I used to tell as a bartender in college.

Somehow, I became aware I was dreaming again, and felt a sense of hope.

I looked to the cash register and saw some daylight coming from a door to the side, and heard the flapping of its blades, faster and faster.

I threw back the rest of the glass of burning peppermint liqueur (just in case I was about to die a horrible death) and ran for it.

My old boss was standing at the door and asked me if I wanted a ride.

What?

He said he had been trying to tell these assholes to stop drinking for years, but none of them would listen.

"Look at them! They're even drinking now!"

"And you have a helicopter outside?"

"Yes! And none of them will get on it.

They're too drunk to realize what's happening! They keep on laughing and telling jokes about helicopters, burning buildings and lawyers every time I mention it!"

"Well, I'm not laughing. Let's go," I said, and we got moving.

We left the building, and ran for the helipad. We jumped into a huge military helicopter that had room for dozens more. As I sat down, I recognized the man sitting next to me. He was very small, and looked to be in his late seventies. He was very well dressed, and wore a trench coat with a matching hat.

"You shouldn't drink," the old man said to me. *He seemed really irritated too, that he even had to tell me.*

FINDING THE FORCE 1:

After a short, uneventful flight, we landed in Albany Airport, safely away from the disaster.

I walked into the airport with Joseph Chilton Pearce. It was then I knew who I had to interview next, if he would even speak to me.

TIP 4: You Have 4 Brains, as well as a Huge Force Field Coming From Your Heart. When You Allow the Force In.

CHAPTER FIVE

Dr. Quantum: Fred Alan Wolfe

He is a letter to Everyone.
You Open it.
It says
"Live!"

-Rumi

Rhinebeck, New York, April 2005

The Omega Institute is a fabulous place for anyone seeking spiritual enlightenment and a good meal. Their instructors feature the best-known people in their fields from all over the world.

Their staff numbers in the hundreds and the campus setting features multiple gardens blossoming with delicious little flowers, green rolling hills and cottages nestled into the greenery.

This weekend's feature seminar was a take-off on *What the Bleep Do We Know?* And was featuring lectures from Masaru Emoto, Fred Alan Wolfe, Joseph Chilton Pearce and Craig Hamilton. Miguel and Jose Ruiz were also doing a weekend seminar on Toltec shamanism and traditions. It felt like a metaphysical candy store, and the Universe had granted me a free pass to stuff myself full.

I really couldn't believe my eyes as I walked around the campus. Golf carts with hippie skirts flittering out the side rushed by, and butterflies landed on picturesque benches. Walking about it is not unusual to see Swamis with turbans engaged in divine bliss, and famous authors and lecturers strolling and chatting.

The oversized dining room offers vegetarian, organic and vegan foods with three meal times. There's also ample space for yoga, meditation and sunning on a lakeside beach. A café offers treats all day and a store sells items related to the lectures and lifestyles purveyed.

Our cozy little cottage gave us a good night's rest and the next day my first mission was to find Fred Alan Wolfe, to make an appointment to speak with him after his lecture.

Wolfe's lecture detailed much of the same material that he covered in '*What the Bleep*' as well s his popular *Dr. Quantum* series. Wolfe gets into a fairly serious level of detail about the space-time continuum and its fluidity, the strange behavior of electrons and the difficulty of pinning down these magnetic building blocks of our reality.

He refers to his experiences with shamanism and yoga, and likes to use the work of Alex Grey to illustrate his points. He makes it all sound simple, and insists that anyone can achieve an understanding of this material, if they pursue it the right way. In

FINDING THE FORCE 1:

fact, Wolfe's books are easy to read, and Dr. Quantum is very easy to understand, though hard to put into practice in a day-to-day type fashion.

He is unusually gruff, and I had to steel myself to the experience of an actual meeting after seeing how he dealt with the attendees' questions. I had sat next to Joe Pearce during the lecture, and this gave me some level of comfort, since he had agreed to speak to me, as well as Patricio Dominguez.

Incidentally, Pearce slept through Fred Wolfe's entire lecture, a point which the reader will want to remember later.

When Wolfe was done answering questions, I approached him and reminded him of our appointment.

He grunted at me and continued speaking to a tall pot-bellied man who was still questioning him as he was trying to escape.

"But, but, wait, Mr. Wolfe!" the large man called out. Wolfe stopped and turned around.

"What?" he replied.

"But, how do I achieve this kind of understanding in my day-to-day life?"

"Yoga, psychedelic drugs or sex."

I couldn't help but laugh at the look on the man's face as Wolfe walked away. At that point I had been beaten up by a lot of people who had refused interviews, and shunned the entire project. I found Wolfe's gruffness a little comforting, and it really wreaked of the typical no bullshit New York attitude.

Then Wolfe turned to gripe at one of the staff members.

"You know, next time, if you want a really good turnout, you should book me exclusively. Nobody else, just me, and you'll have ten times the turnout." (The room had been packed with over a hundred people…)

The young woman looked a little taken aback but she nodded her head and smiled. They must be used to some real characters rolling through there.

So we began walking away together, and walked quietly.

As we were approaching the café, where we had agreed to meet another fan approached, this time wanting to pawn a video tape off on the guy. She was young and eager to speak to him, and really genuinely excited.

"Mr. Wolfe! Did you know that there are people working miracles with The Course in Miracles?"

"A Course in Miracles? I didn't know there were even people still using that thing." With that he started to walk away.

"But, wait! I have a tape for you! They are making profound healings with it!"

"There's no way I can accept a tape. I just don't have room in my suitcase for all the things people want to hand me. I am sure that they are doing great things with it, and I am happy for you."

She didn't look excited anymore as we walked away. I felt bad for her, but glad to see his style and know what I was in for.

We sat down at a table by a window and Wolfe pulled out his laptop and began checking his e-mail. He completely ignored me.

I sat and looked out the window and waited. I ate some chocolate and reminded myself that in many situations, she who speaks first loses. I made like a cat and ate quietly.

After some time it was clear that he was just going to continue to ignore me, and I asked if he was ready.

"Ready for what? What do you want?" he said, still looking at his e-mail.

"I want to speak to you about your work, and about your knowledge. I have spoken with a number of people and am compiling interviews to put together into a book about consciousness and the end of this time cycle. It focuses on scientific research and Indigenous Traditions mainly."

FINDING THE FORCE 1:

That was my standard boilerplate reply when anyone asked me what I was doing. I had it memorized so I wouldn't panic and stutter and make a fool of myself.

Wolfe sat there staring at my chocolate bar, not answering.

"Are you OK?"

"Yes, but I have a problem with chocolate."

"You can have some."

"No, I've had too much already. Look at my belly."

"You're fine. You should have some. I would be happy to share it," I said breaking off a few pieces.

"Well, OK, I'll take it, but only because I'm a nice Jewish boy who likes to be fed."

"That should work out nicely since I'm a nice Jewish mother who's in the business of feeding people."

"So what's going on?" Wolfe inquired.

I was looking out the window again, wondering what to say. I figured time was short, so I better get to the point.

"Aside from the research for the novel, what I am doing is trying to figure out what's going on with me. You see, I have been having some really strange dreams where a daughter that I don't have is talking to me. She says she's from the future, and that in order for her to get born I have to write a book and come speak to certain people. Pearce, Dominguez, Emoto…You're one of them too. So, is that possible or am I just losing my mind?"

"Of course it is. That's no big deal at all. Space time is fluid and in a certain state you can communicate across time with no problem. So what else is she telling you?"

"Oh, just that the sky is falling and we better get ourselves back to the garden. She's showing me an eco-spiritual community based on the Tree of Life, where the survivors of some kind of global turmoil found a home."

"Interesting. Well, you better get yourself in The Flow, and keep it up if you want her to be born." He looked back at his computer.

I handed him some more chocolate, like trying to put more quarters into a talking meter with fuzzy hair and glasses.

"What's The Flow?"

"It's a place both inside and outside of time, where the mind can go."

"How do I know when I'm there?"

"It's like sex. You can be having sex, and getting off, and then you have a thought, and you're not getting off anymore. It's like that. You just know. If you have to ask, you're not there. And if you're there and you ask if you are, you're not."

"So can I use a Merkaba, like Drunvalo Melchizedek says? Can I activate my heart-mind connection like Pearce says? What about the Central Pillar of the Tree of Life? Will that get me there?" I was fishing to see if anything I was presently doing would work if I just kept it up. I felt a little bewildered, and I was glad I had heard his response to the big guy after his lecture before about sex drugs and yoga.

"Look, forget about Drunvalo and the Merkaba, forget about Pearce and the Heart. Just read Dr. Quantum and get into the Flow. Once you're there in the Flow, you can do whatever you need to do. Are we done yet?"

I was all out of chocolate. The meter was redlining.

"Yep. We're done. Thanks."

I felt strangely happy as I left the café. I felt like someone had given me some really important information.

And I laughed about Pearce sleeping through Wolfe's lecture.

Forget about Pearce and the Heart. That would be hard to do, but the Flow, Finding The Force, might just get me what I needed anyhow.

The afternoon speeches came fast after my meeting with Wolfe, and the campus was just as lovely in the afternoon as the morning. Especially in the spring light, it was glowing an otherworldly green. There were little golf carts with staff flying around everywhere. Walking along rubbing elbows with world famous authors, yogis, shaman was so stimulating and intellectual, but I still almost expected to look up and see elves perched in the trees and gnomes popping out of a garden path. Or maybe that's who was driving the golf carts. No, those were just colorful

FINDING THE FORCE 1:

skirts flapping in the wind, attached to bare-bellied hippies with streaming hair. Similar feeling though, halfway between Narnia and Oxford.

In any event, I had to run off quickly and find the building where Pearce would be speaking. As he had said, he would be speaking on the Heart-Mind connection, and he was known as a fantastic lecturer.

Nothing prepares you, though, to see an older man in his eighties, transformed into a glowing figure, moving about the stage, and slapping his hands, whacking the board with a stick, and getting himself worked up over the implications of the research he has done.

I was not anticipating how moving Joseph Chilton Pearce's speech would be. He had seemed rather subdued and nervous in person, and his falling asleep during Wolfe's lecture seemed apropos once I saw him in action.

Though I had been obsessed with his writing on childrearing and brain development, his new work really had a lot more to do with my research. He spoke about the connection between the different areas of the brain, and how things connect to the heart.

Surprisingly, the heart has been shown to actually be more like brain tissue than a muscle. In fact, according to Pearce, the Heart is *the ultimate brain.* Once the two sides of the brain are synched up and our mind is quiet, then the heart takes over and begins to run things. A quote from Pearce in an interview online (http://www.appliedmeditation.org/The_Heart/articles_joseph_chilton_pearce.shtml):

> *Quite literally, in other words, there is a "brain" in the heart, whose ganglia are linked to every major organ in the body, to the entire muscle spindle system that uniquely enables humans to express their emotions. About half of the heart's neural cells are involved in translating information sent to it from all over the body so that it can keep the body working as one harmonious whole. And the other half make up a very large, unmediated neural connection with the emotional brain in our head and carry on a twenty-four-hour-a-day dialogue between the heart and the brain that we are not even aware of.*

FINDING THE FORCE 1

In a sense, we become super human when we can develop a good connection between our hearts and our brains (vis-à-vis our emotions), and mold our reality through our emotions. The brain can be used to send messages to the heart, which will in turn generate the response that one has sent. The heart does not determine how we feel, but rather, it produces the hormonal results that the brain mandates, without qualifying the sense of it. That's what the brain is supposed to be doing!

But instead, when we are under stress, or have not received the proper stimulation and nourishing as children, we have a constant recorder playing in our brains, mixed with fears, worries, doubts, as well as unsatisfied needs that stress us out and depress us. Until we can quiet the brain's storyteller (as Ruiz puts it) we are not really in control. What the Bleep eloquently demonstrates how this looks – we are our animal side, controlled by hormonal rushes and limbic brain fears that keep us running like gerbils on a treadmill. The owner of the brain and heart need not be aware of their condition in order to be in it. In fact, that's often how it works. We are embedded in it, and not aware, and that's exactly what keeps us from realizing our potential. Perhaps the very framework of society perpetuates this mind-state with its materialism and alarmist media hype. We are all terrified every time we turn on a TV, whether we know it or not. Every time our brains see violence, there is a bodily response, and it perpetuates a cycle of fear, anxiety and tension, making us blind to our surroundings and higher nature.

Another quote from Pearce will help to illustrate:

> *In other words, the responses that the heart makes affect the entire human system. Meanwhile, biophysicists have discovered that the heart is also a very powerful electromagnetic generator. It creates an electromagnetic field that encompasses the body and extends out anywhere from eight to twelve feet away from it.*
>
> *It is so powerful that you can take an electrocardiogram reading from as far as three feet away from the body.*

The field the heart produces is holographic, meaning that you can read it from any point on the body and from any point within the field.

FINDING THE FORCE 1:

No matter how microscopic the sample is, you can receive the information of the entire field.

> *The intriguing thing is how profoundly this electromagnetic field affects the brain. All indications are that it furnishes the whole radio wave spectrum from which the brain draws its material to create our internal experience of the world.*

Many Aboriginal and Indigenous Peoples believed that there is a large field that surrounds the body that actually creates our reality here. Ancients believed that reality if fluid, and that our singular response molds our experience, and that our collective experience shapes our world. They practiced meditation, and all kinds of yoga in order to clear the mind and liberate the body to fulfill their higher potential, their destiny. The key has always been to remove chronic tension from the musculo-skeletal system at the same time as quieting mind-babble, thus allowing the heart-field to expand.

This heart mind field is spherical, and as Pearce states, reaches out beyond the body by about 8-10 feet. The Ancients also mentioned yet another level of spherical field, extending to more than 50 feet, known as the Merkaba, or Light Body Vehicle. This was the ultimate vehicle to mold reality, and according to legend is the computer that generates the very fabric of reality, by sending pseudo-electrical pulses down through denser and denser fields, until they finally manifest as our earthly bodies.

Though these legends sound preposterous at a glance, they sound a lot truer once one hears that there are layers of electromagnetic fields, in the heart, and then a larger bubble surrounding the smaller one in the heart.

According to Pearce, our society and our very culture have created the problems that stunt our growth, intellectual, emotional and spiritual. When asked what we can do to help our children, especially teenagers, Pearce replied:

> *Well, first of all a great many teenagers have no idea what their desires are because they haven't been given the opportunity to find out. So, we can start by helping them to identify their desires.*

FINDING THE FORCE 1

Next, we can start being more proactive rather than reactionary. Most of the crises that are occurring in our young people today are arbitrary, that is they're created by the culture itself. Instead of spending millions of dollars trying to fix what's wrong with teens we should invest in educating people to be good parents, to love and nurture their babies and young children so they don't have huge problems later on. The first four years of life are the most important. In Sweden, new mothers are given three years of maternity leave. It used to be one, and now they've upped it to three so that mothers can stay home with their children. And they're giving fathers a one-year leave of absence with full pay so that both mother and father can be with their child for the first critical year. So when you ask what can we do with our teenagers, I say we can begin by preventing the damage right from the very beginning...

There are some extraordinary things happening right now, in little pockets all over the world, examples of true coherency in a massively incoherent system. And when this global economy nightmare we've unleashed finally self-destructs – as I think it has to –these small pockets of coherent intelligence will then manifest themselves and provide the impetus and the wisdom for the changes necessary to create a world in which children can reach their full potential. I am very optimistic about this.

Sounds a lot like a World Womb. What if someone or something was trying to speak through me?

Maybe my unborn daughter was trying to lead me to become aware of children's needs, and the greater human need to unlock our potential?

Maybe our planet itself would be raising the bar for the required standard to exist here.

Gaia was rolling over in her sleep, and starting a new dream, a beautiful one. I felt like I had passed a test with the nightmare of the Howling Wolf Man, like I had made a deep connection between my heart and my brain, and that this was an important piece of why I had not been eaten.

FINDING THE FORCE 1:

I still wondered though, why was the Wolf Man coming after me, of all people? According to many cultures, dreams are something that trying to convey a deeper truth to us. Sometimes they can be messages. If so, what was the Wolf Man trying to tell me?

As I was falling asleep hoping that my dreams would get better, I looked at the book on my stand and wondered if there was a connection between Fred Alan Wolfe and my dream.

Had I somehow gotten into "The Flow" in the dreamtime when I had to face the Wolf?

TRIP 5: DREAM OF THE HOWLING WOLF MAN

He is a letter to Everyone.
You Open it.
It says
"Live!"

-Rumi

New York, April 2005

The vivid dreams continued for some time. There was only one that ever scared me, a real nightmare, and I cannot remember having ever awakened in such a state of terror in my life, even as a child. I was being hunted by the Howling Wolf-Man.

I am pregnant once again, very much so, that late stage of pregnancy where one really doesn't even want to walk.
And I had to run. Fast.

I woke up into the dream world in a dark studio apartment. I was looking out the windows onto these ancient looking streets. The back gave out onto a huge garden area, almost like a public park, but

FINDING THE FORCE 1

very elegant, full of fountains and flowers and mosaic covered sculptures in bright color.

But for some reason I was looking out onto the streets, and the shadows were moving around in a bad way.

I couldn't see anyone on the streets, but the shadows were moving about. They were moving around way too much, in ways that didn't look very human. The shadows were darting about, looking for something. They were looking for something to eat.

And I could hear what it was thinking. It was very hungry, very ancient, very very wild, like a force of nature, of another order. I had this horrible feeling that there was no point in running, and that's exactly what it wanted me to think. And that's when I hit it as fast as I could for the back door. When I turned to look back as I heard the shattering of glass, it was standing in my living room where I had just been looking out on the streets.

Its head and ears nearly touched the ceiling and it was dripping from the mouth. I remember so vividly what the teeth looked like, and I knew it was looking to use them on me. And especially my baby, still in my belly. I could see that it wanted the baby.

There is no fear in the world like that of being pregnant and having to run because something is trying to eat your belly. I have to be honest, it was like being shot up with something, and I have to say, it made me really superhuman fast. And I was aware of just how very much I needed to be calm, to be in a higher state of awareness, if I was going to escape the Wolf Man.

And he knew that too. He could also hear me, hear what I was thinking and feeling. He wasn't even running after me, he was standing in my living room, howling. He was howling in a way that was mind-numbing. It rattled through every bone, muscle and or ligament. It was like a mind-eraser. I had to figure out how I was going to calm myself down in the middle of these shockwaves of horror.

I had the weird sensation too, in the dream world, that he knew exactly the effect it had, and that he was sending his intentions the sound waves.

FINDING THE FORCE 1:

I could feel his will penetrate my body. I dropped to the ground and prayed that me and my child would be safe, that we would have the chance to have a life together, get to know each other, love each other.

And I think it was that dream that was making the Wolf Man feel so hungry.

It wanted to not only eat my child, but eat my dreams forever. It wanted to devour the very part of me the dreamed those dreams. And it was totally cold and indifferent, like it was just business. It was its only purpose. To eat things.

When my body hit the ground I was beginning to feel better. I could really hear something talking to me. It told me exactly what to do. It showed me how I was going to get myself out of this. I was going to have to find complete peace, be totally centered, be unafraid.

I was going to lift myself into a higher state of being. The only way out was to kind of sublimate, make myself 'lighter' and not subject to the normal laws of reality - not that Wolf Man came from any normal reality. But I had to realize that I didn't have to obey the normal laws either. In the dreamtime anything can happen

As I gathered my strength, the howling started even stronger, and I felt I had to sit down on the earth and ground myself, and I felt the earth itself absorbing some of the shock of the waves of terror the Wolf Man was sending out.

Getting more and more in touch with the strength of the land, and whatever thoughts and ideas were behind it, I found that I was able to tap into some higher strengths and powers that we all have. Maybe it's only in times of crisis, maybe only in nightmares, or in Hollywood, but it came. Before long I was standing in the middle of the garden, in front of the fountain, and I was blindfolded. It was something within me I was supposed to understand, something beyond the fear and adrenaline. And it was very still thing, like the moonlight, like the flowers. I was sure it was going to eat me and the cops in the real world would find my dead body on the side of the road, half eaten. I just accepted it.

Really I wanted to just know if there was something beyond that, something beyond our physical life. And it seemed like it was there, like a tapestry beyond normal reality. It was like a thought form that was

FINDING THE FORCE 1

within everything, that was the building block of everything. It was something like a loving parent, truly, truly something vast enough and simple enough to drench every part of me. Things slowed, baubles of light moved through everything.

Once I released my attachment to the situation, everything shifted. I knew that Wolf Man would devour me eventually, but if I had it my way, today would not be that day. I released my fear of death, fear of my baby dying, fear of everything always going wrong.

And when I did, I became much stronger. I actually went back inside and looked for the Wolf. It was still howling. Still big. Still reeally hairy. But nothing was going to stop me from having my shot at him. I was determined to make it happen my way, and not check out because I was too afraid to face it. The teeth came flying at me from the other side of the room, attached to a jaw like a grizzly bear. Halfway across the room, though, something flew at it from the very wall itself.

A cat had emerged from nowhere, and was attacking the face of the Wolf Man. It had not seen it coming and it was clawing in a surprising fierce was at his eyes. He couldn't get it off of him, and it was really doing some damage. The blood and fur was flying like a B movie. And there I was, watching it all take place. Like a dream. Right?

Having drawn the Wolf Man's attention away, the cat jumped out the open window into the night. With a final howl, of course, the Wolf Man flew out the window after it. And, also of course, I did wake up screaming.

TIP 5: The Flow, the Dao, the Force, is the quiet space between, the Silence, the Vortex of Power. We Drop into the Force when we allow Conscious, Non-Dual Connection to the Unseen. ------------------------------
----

FINDING THE FORCE 1:
CHAPTER SIX

Jose and Miguel Ruiz:

Soul receives from soul that knowledge,
therefore not by book
nor from tongue.
If knowledge of mysteries
come after emptiness of mind,
that is illumination of heart.

- Rumi

Rhinebeck NY, Omega Institute, April 2005

Miguel Ruiz is a Toltec shaman. It's not easy to understand what that means, because it's so far away from our day-to-day reality. I once thought I knew what a shaman was, but after the experience of speaking with a few, I have my doubts as to how much I can really understand it all.

They have told me that in fact, the word *nagual* is a better word to use than shaman, especially in Ruiz's case. *Nagual* means master, but since the times of Castaneda, we have been reading about what *naguales* do, and some of their abilities and claims are quite extraordinary.

The Toltec were a group of people who were known in Mexico thousands of years ago as "women and men of knowledge".

According to Ruiz,
"The Toltec were scientists and artists who formed a society to explore and conserve spiritual knowledge and practices of the ancient ones."

Ruiz is essentially a master of spiritual knowledge and his books are well-known around the world, and quoted frequently by students and researchers alike.

FINDING THE FORCE 1

To read about some of the powers of naguales and shaman is something, but to meet one in real life is completely different than reading about it.

If you are reading about it, you can say to yourself, "Wow that sounds neat, wish it were true," but you are not confronted with the real possibility that it IS true, that human beings are actually capable of extraordinary feats. A person can sit and read about these things and slough it off, but when you are sitting in front of them speaking, feeling, I mean knowing, that you are completely transparent and they are wise beyond your comprehension, it's a very different matter.

Patricio Dominguez, who the reader met in the first chapter, and Miguel Ruiz are completely "normal" intelligent and collected people. They looked me straight in the eye as we spoke, and were extremely observant, present, and conscious. Unnervingly so, I would add. Nothing I spoke to them about confused, alarmed or concerned them, except perhaps to comment on some interesting details in my paintings.

I looked them both straight in the face at more than one point and asked if it were really possible that an unborn daughter from the future was trying to communicate important messages to me about how to construct an ideal society where we could all escape the impending doom of global warming and the end of Time.

Neither of them flinched. In fact, they seemed a little perkier – like it was good news that someone was paying attention.

FINDING THE FORCE 1:

After many years of trying to explain myself to friends and family members, I have become accustomed to reactions that range from peals of laughter to looks of disdain and disgust. I was even asked why I bothered to go to college if I was going to go out and waste my life this way. Most people just stopped inviting me to their parties, let's say.

But to these naguales, this is completely possible and even desirable. In fact, they looked at me very seriously when I started to explain myself, and seemed more and more interested the more and more I explained the story.

So, after I got done speaking with Masaru Emoto, I went to find Miguel and Jose Ruiz. Jose is Miguel's son, and he is his student, and replacement, so to speak. Before I had a chance to speak with Don Miguel, Jose was kind enough to spend some time with me.

Jose is about medium sized, with very long wavy black hair, and a beautiful face full of light. The best way to find Jose is to look for the guy hugging everyone.

I mean it. Every single person he comes up to, he hugs, and not just a little. He actually really embraces people, and holds them in his arms for a few moments. I'm a pretty affectionate person but, I was a little nervous about the procedure.

When I arrived at the area where the Ruizes were conducting their seminar, I snuck in quietly to catch the end. Jose Ruiz was speaking to the group, who all had their eyes closed, saying something like:

Imagine that you are swimming in that beautiful lake out there on a sunny day, and the water is cool and fresh.

FINDING THE FORCE 1

You are swimming together with everyone here and you are so happy. In some moment you begin to feel that you are one with the lake, that you are part of it, and it is part of you.

Then you look up and notice that the sun is shining on the lake, twinkling and making little dances on the waves. You notice that this light is also part of the lake, and you are part of it too.

Looking around at everyone's faces, you feel that you are one with them too, and that everything is actually love. You are swimming in the lake, and the lake is light, the water is light and love, and you are one with it, and one with everyone else. I am swimming in you, and I am Love. You are swimming in me and you are Love too...

Frankly, I was entranced. I have never forgotten the feeling coming off that room, and looking out at the lake behind Jose Ruiz, with the sun sparkling on it, feeling that I was part of something massively grand.

In that moment, I had no doubt about anything I was doing or feeling, nor (for once) did I question my existence, and all kinds of restless yearnings abated.

When the moment faded away, the group broke and I approached Jose.

Of course when I walked up to him, before I could even explain myself, the first order of business was a bear hug. It seemed to last forever, and I found myself squirming. He peeked around my shoulder to look at me funny, and re engaged in the procedure. He kept on hugging until he was reasonably sure I had calmed down, and then looked at me.

I felt better than I had in years. It was amazing.

I had wanted just that kind of hug, full of something inexpressibly fuzzy and bright, all my life. I felt I was home. I cannot explain it to you for it is an experiential matter. I highly recommend it. He just gives them out for free all over the place.

As I was walking with Jose and a group of his students, he broke out in song. He likes Ozzy Osbourne and just started singing "Mamma I'm Coming Home!!" and then laughed happily. It was really cool.

FINDING THE FORCE 1:

After the students dispersed, I began by asking Jose about Earth Changes, and what he knew. He said next to nothing, and told me that I'd have to speak to his father about that.

I asked about his father's work, and apologized, as I had not read it because I was not planning on this interview.

He explained *The Four Agreements* by saying that out there in the world we choose what we want to experience. Most people are part of a bad dream, a nightmare that's pretty much planetary. It's passed down from parent to child, without people realizing it.

"What are the Four Agreements," I inquired.

"*Be Impeccable With Your Word*," he smiled.

"OK. Got that," I replied.

"*Never Take Anything Personally*," he nodded.

"Fair enough," I said.

"Let me see. Huh. The third one is *Always Do Your Best*. No wait, that's four", he said stopping to think.

I looked at him and giggled, thinking it was a little bit funny that he couldn't remember his father's shamanic teachings from one to four.

Jose also laughed and he just let it go.

"Oh well, it's not important. He says that just with the first one you can completely transform your life. You should read the book. It's really good."

"Well, so, what about the dream of the planet?" I asked as we were walking around. I was actually trying to take him to find my portfolio and couldn't find my room.
So I was hardly in a place to be balking about the Fourth Agreement missing.

"Oh, the dream of the planet is a bad nightmare. But", he said, "Just like the bee, we can choose where to fly to. The bee can go to honey, to the flowers, or the bee can waste its life stinging and throw away its true purpose. It's our choice too, just like that."

"So you are saying the same thing, as everybody else – We manifest our existence here," I replied. I have to admit I was tired of hearing that line, and was really hoping someone was going to give me more specific instructions and secret insider knowledge so I could save the world really quick.

FINDING THE FORCE 1

"Yes, but its more than that," and he smiled.

Still, I wasn't buying it and I let him know.

"Alright then, so, we are creating this reality here for ourselves, according to you. Don't you think if that were true that more people would manifest something nicer? I mean, do you think people really want to be involved in murder, and war, and hatred every day? C'mon, if we had a choice, we wouldn't do that."

"We do have a choice. Each one of us chooses what kind of experience we want," he insisted.

"But then what am I supposed to do when I go out there into the world the way it is?" I said, still wanting to know what the real trick was.

"You have to decide what kind of experience you want and go after it. If someone else chooses something different, alright, that's their choice. You can't control that, but you just don't get stuck in it.

Like me for instance. I am so happy. I feel sad sometimes, too, but really, I am just so happy. You know what I feel like?" Jose asked.

"What?" I was feeling a little disgusted and cynical. These guys didn't have mortgages and kids and reality to deal with. He was some famous guy and he got to travel around all the time. Of course he was happy. It was annoying.

But I bit my tongue and listened. I kept thinking about Masaru Emoto's work, about the power of thought and the power of the word, and I thought Jose might just be right.

"I feel like I am on vacation all the time. Every day I wake up and I feel like I am on vacation. I am grateful to be alive, and that is the dream I choose too dream. You get to choose yours too. What will you choose?" he ended, quite pleased with himself.

Standing there looking at him, there was something contagious. He was beautiful, and happy and sharing that with others. And he was completely sincere. And a Rumi poem popped into my head that I had been reading:

'Soul receives from soul that knowledge, therefore not by book nor from tongue...'

Masters pass their wisdom on by just being around their students, in some ways. Though Ruiz's words were powerful, it was really his presence and his embrace that affected me.

FINDING THE FORCE 1:

The truth is, no matter how cynical I was at that moment, Jose Ruiz gave me a great gift that day. He changed my life because he changed my dream of my life. As ridiculous as this may seem, every morning I wake up now, I tell myself:

I am happy and grateful to be alive. I feel like I am on vacation. I will fly to the honey.

And it has come truer and truer each day. You should try it too.

Jose was telling the truth.

After I got done walking with Jose, we meandered over to the cafeteria where his father was waiting. Don Miguel Ruiz had recently suffered a heart attack that took the majority of his heart's muscle tissue, and so he was very quiet, and scooting around in a wheelchair, to save what was left.

When we were all done eating, Miguel Ruiz gestured for me that it was time to come over.

He said, "I have a plane to catch so I only have fifteen minutes to talk to you and no matter how much I would like to I cannot extend the time any further."

I got out my notepad and pen and got ready to write.

"Well, I am a freelance journalist working on a novel about Earth Changes and Ancient Traditions. I'd like to talk about 2012."

"What about it," he replied matter of fact-ly.

"What's going to happen?"

"Nothing. December 31st 2012 will be a day just like any other day," he told me.

"Nothing will happen?"

"Nothing at all. Is that it?" he asked looking at me expressionless.

"Well, uh no," I said taken aback.

Dominguez had said that the changes that were coming were going to escalate until that time, and then de-escalate on the other side of that day, like 2012 was just the peak of a wave, and we would go up and down either side equally. So, I kind of understood how it was possible that 2012 wouldn't be a big event.

My mind was going blank, and all the important questions I had to ask him had abandoned me to be a complete idiot, all alone.

I felt that weird naked feeling again, like he could see through me into my deepest heart of hearts. I felt like a fraud. Was I really a journalist? Who the hell was I to be asking this important man these questions?

I resisted the urge to flee.

"Well, what is the most important thing do can do to heal the world?"

"People should stop telling lies," Ruiz said.

Oh no! He knows I'm a fraud.

Run! Run away! Liar! He knows! Run!

"Lies? What do you mean?" I asked.

"Lies. That people should stop telling lies. All kinds of lies. About everything," Ruiz replied.

Now that I have read all his work thoroughly, I understand what he's talking about. Ruiz teaches that we have all been indoctrinated into a world of lies, into the nightmare of the planet. He teaches that none of this is true and that we need not suffer this way.

But people have been passing their pain on to their children for millennia now, and it's difficult to escape. That's what The Four Agreements and Mastery of Love are about. How to escape.

Ruiz looked at me with my portfolio sitting there and said, "Look, if you want to ask me some questions you better get on with it. As I told you, I have to go in ten minutes and afterwards you might feel disappointed if you don't get to the point. I don't want that to happen to you."

"OK fine. I need to ask you some questions about some weird dreams I have been having."

"That's' more like it," he replied and seemed to gain some interest.

FINDING THE FORCE 1:

I explained everything, just as I had to Don Patricio Dominguez in the end. About the daughter taking me around the World Womb, about the raven, and about needing to make the interviews so she could get born.

"It would take many hundreds of years to build an ideal society. You should go home now to your family and take care of them. Nothing is going to happen," he said.

Only a nagual could get away with telling someone to go home and cook.

But what was I going to do? Accuse him of being a chauvinist? I only had seven minutes, so I didn't bother.

"OK then. Let's talk about these paintings," I retorted and unzipped the portfolio. "These paintings really bother me until I get them done. There is one for each interview and I take them to the person and they explain it. My daughter gives me the painting in my dreams and tells me who to go see."

"Yes..."

"Here," I said "What's this one about?"

Ruiz's face didn't change at all, despite the exploding vagina scene. He finally raised an eyebrow and said he really liked it.

"This above her head is the Old Energies. This is Gaia giving birth to the New Energies. The circles up top here above her head are me, and the ones down below are my son," he said.

"And what about these little critters hopping around?"

"Those are her helpers."

"*Duendes*, right?"

"Yes," he said.

Duendes are little spirit allies that a shaman uses to aid in different workings. They are supposed to be nature spirits that only the trained can see and communicate with."

"And you can see in those shapes behind her there is a Merkaba, and they are her energy body, full of light," I said.

"Yes, because things are shifting, and much light is coming in," Ruiz noted.

I also showed him the one I had given to Don Patricio, and he explained it.

"You are the bird there, drinking from the water in the pitcher. Your path is open to you, right up those stairs. Whatever your mission is, you can achieve it."

"But how?" I asked.

"Just fly. Fly right out the window, little bird. Up, up and out the window," Ruiz said.

He made a gesture with his hand, and I could feel a piece of me shift, and fly out that window. Like in the dream.

At the time all I could think is that he was completely right. There was that bird sitting there, and it was obvious that it was about to fly up and out. Over time I was able to use his words to convince myself that I was powerful enough to do this, and it has kept me going during even the hardest of times.

I also showed Ruiz something I've never talked about with anyone before.

When you turn my painting of the Raven upside down, there is a creature hiding there that looks like an alien. And I knew it was there for a reason, trying to tell me something.

"What is that there?" and I pointed to the creature upside down in the painting. It kept bothering me because I felt like it was looking at me, even when the painting was turned right side up.

"Is that a Star Ancestor?"

"One kind," he said.

"And why is it there?" I asked.

"Because that's what you were before you came here," he told me.

What was I going to say to that?

I also told him about the horrible Wolf nightmare I had when I was carrying Adrian.

"I kept on having this dream that a wolf creature is trying to devour my baby. It comes after me in a tiny room, and it's going for my baby. It's huge and terrifying, I can even see the saliva on nits teeth as it's about to eat up my belly."

FINDING THE FORCE 1:

"Yes," he replied completely calm.

"Well, why is it trying to eat my baby?"

"Because knowledge is the Wolf. Eventually knowledge eats everyone, and your baby is no exception," said Ruiz.

"But why is knowledge the wolf?" I asked.

"Because that's the way it is in Gaia's dream," Ruiz said.

He got up then and took the paintings with him that I had given him. He was truly grateful and he even said he really liked them a lot.

"Goodbye. Good luck with everything," Ruiz said, and turned and departed.

"Thanks."

All I could do was just stand there and watch him go. Moments like those never come again, and I was glad I had stuck it out and asked what I really wanted to.

As I looked in his eyes, I remembered why he looked so familiar. Those dancing eyes.

The keeper of the Butterfly Lotus of Light.

What a day.

TRIP 6: DREAM OF THE BUTTERFLY LOTUS

New York, April 2005

In the Dreamtime I am skipping and flying across a moonlight night terrain. My feet lightly touch the ground over the forest growth, and I glide easily through the trees, the brush and the flowers until I sense that I must slow down. Before me soon comes

FINDING THE FORCE 1

a deep gorge, with water flowing somewhere deep down at the rocky bottom.

I sense clearly that on the other side of the ravine I something vitally important, it is calling me. A teacher, a master of such grace that the sweetness of that honey golden light is dancing on the leaves of the forest, flickering the way a fire's light would. I can see that dancing light from the distance, and though I do not know exactly what it holds for me, I know this is my chance to find my destiny.

But the gap between me and the other side is clearly so huge that no one could cross it without a bridge. I don't have time to make a bridge! And crossing down bottom would take days.

It comes down to this. Do I really believe that I can fly, or not?

I decide that I can. That I must.

I skip backwards into the forest, to give it a running head start, gain a little momentum. I am practically flying by the time I get back to the edge and I take a huge leap.

I begin to sink for a moment as my feet search for solid ground to push off of, and then, I hear myself ask once again,

Do I really believe that I can fly, or not?

When the answer comes, yes, I begin to lift, a little, then a little more, a little more, and then it's as if I am riding a surfboard through the air, my feet are pressing against something gently, and I am propelled forward.

I can comfortably look down, and far below see the white foam of the rapids, see the moonlight reflect off of the rushing waters. But I focus mostly on that honey colored light up ahead, far in the distance.

FINDING THE FORCE 1:

When I arrive, I land in the forest before the clearing that the light is coming from. There is a master sitting on a wooden stump, before the semi circle of students seated cross-legged on the earth. Before I even arrive, the master senses me, and I sense the clear thought of Welcome.

The students all look different, but each is wrapped in a special blanket, a hand woven one, suited to them uniquely. The master has brown skin and very short hair, dark, dancing eyes.

The golden light is coming from a huge lotus blossom sitting in front of the master. It is being held open in full bloom, through the life connection between the flower and the master. He is using the flower as a teaching tool. The students are duly impressed.

As I approach I see that he is handing them their own lotus blossoms, which they take in turn in their hands. When the small pink bud touches their hand, it seems to express some quality or state of the mind that holds them. Each flower does something different, depending upon the thoughts or feelings of the students.

I watch carefully from the edge of the clearing, not wanting to interrupt, and also wanting to study the activity and understand on my own. Again, the master with the dancing eyes pulls a baby lotus out of the large one which glows golden. He holds it in his hand, holds a thought, and the flower responds. It opens its delicate flowers and stays open, then begins to shine a golden light such as the Mother Lotus in front of it.

As they light fades, the petals fall off and blow away.

The students try again. Each one holds a flower in their hand.

Some shrivel without lighting up, some dance a little, a few flicker with a sparkling light, one even pops in a shower of golden dust.

The master laughs happily, pleased with their efforts. They are making the connection between their thoughts and emotions, and the manifest

FINDING THE FORCE 1

world. Way up here, high up on a mountain, in the moonlight, they are closer to higher consciousness, closer to the mental plane of reality.

Finally the master's eyes come to rest on me. Even though I am still standing outside of the ring of light from the lotus, he can see me. I don't think it's his eyes he is using!

I come over and am invited to join the circle, and a blanket is lifted in welcome.

The Eye of God symbol is woven all over it.

The master looks so familiar, now that I am close. Especially those eyes.

He indicates that I should open my hands, and reaches into the huge Mother Lotus of golden light. He pulls out a new round of blossoms and distributes them, this time, only one at a time.

The students are improving quickly, as they correlate between their thoughts and the appearance of the blossoms. First and most essential they must clear their minds and keep them clear. That seems to allow the blossom time to adjust to its new situation, and make a good connection mentally. Once the mind of the student is held clear, the blossom lights up from within.

Many of the students capture that part, and can get synchronized enough to open the light channel. But no one seems sure what the next step is, because after that, it is purely a matter of choice. Since they are unsure what the next step is, the petals mostly just fall off and make a beautiful show.

But I am bugged over it, because I can't stand it, to not be able to take the next step. What is the next step anyhow? It is all so personal to each one of us, but if one is to spend all the time and energy it requires to achieve some sort of enlightenment, then the next step after it has to be of vital importance.

FINDING THE FORCE 1:

For all the spiritual training we do, and everything we sacrifice, what are we really gaining?

I open my hands. Everything is darkness except for that sweetness, that light that comes from the jewel-like center of that lotus. It seems like a very long time that I am one with its Beauty, and I remember the stories of goddesses like Sarasvati emerging from a pool of golden amrita (spiritual nectar). That amrita must come from the beautiful thoughts and emotions of human beings, and other creatures, who render their consciousness into the pool of divine adoration.

My mind is completely clear. When I begin to think, to analyze what the next step is, the blossom sparks some, and fades.

"Pásame otra flor por favor."

Mind clear.

This flower is one of exquisite beauty, burgundy, pink, red, white and violet, with a many many faceted jewel in its center.

I am completely merged into its grace, and I realize, with some amazement,

"I am a part of that!"

When that moment of joy penetrates me, and I realize that I am a piece of that Joy and Love, the golden light begins to saturate me, it soaks into my hands first, and when I look down I see that the light is glowing from my heart too, and soon, my throat and brow.

A strange sort of music begins to play, to emerge, and perhaps I was the only one who could hear it, because they were all staring at the flower, it was getting ready to do something altogether different.

FINDING THE FORCE 1

I remember sensing that I was in the Flow.

What next?

We were all glowing that honey sweet light then, when the petals of the flower in my hands transformed into butterfly wings, and thousands of tiny butterflies danced up into the night sky.

And everything was perfect Love.

TIP 6: Cleansing Wrong Thinking and Trauma through Self Awareness was a large part of Toltec Shamanic Wisdom.

CHAPTER SEVEN

Masaru Emoto: Water Crystal

If in thirst, you drink
water from a cup
You see God in It.
Those who do not Love God
see only themselves.
-Rumi

The Omega Institute, April 2005 *"What the Bleep Do We Know"* **Conference**

FINDING THE FORCE 1:

Masaru Emoto is a Japanese physician who began studying water many years ago as part of his healing practice. Many people have heard of his work, as his novel is an international best-seller. He also was featured in *"What the Bleep Do We Know?"* and so was part of the same conference as Pearce and Wolfe. He was the last person I was scheduled to see in the conference.

When Emoto began to suspect that water had many secrets, he found ways of trying to get it to share. He began freezing water and looking at it under microscopes and found something amazing. No two water crystals were alike from different samples. He wondered what affected their structure and knew how important the integrity of water was, since water comprises more than seventy percent of a mature human body.

As he started to look at these breathtaking photos of water crystals, he began to suspect that the mind and the waters' environment had an effect on the structure of water. If this hypothesis were true, it would be an incredible discovery, since water is the single most important part of our existence here.

Not only is our body made mostly of water, but also our planet. The way that water molecules bond together changes the properties of water, and changes the quality of the water carrier, that is, human beings.

In its liquid state water is of course, just that, fluid. But when frozen it forms a specific kind of crystalline structure that reflects the state it was in when frozen.

Water molecules take on a certain type of structure due to their electro-magnetic composition. It's a little bit like making a snowflake pattern out of magnets, and it looks somewhat like a Star of David, or a Merkaba. Healthy water molecules bond together to form two overlapping equilateral triangles - a six-pointed figure. It looks much like the frost crystals seen around the edges of windows on a cold winter morning. He started by looking at water from different areas, and noticed that some crystals were irregular or formless.

Emoto then did experiments with water to see what kind of effect words would have on it. When he taped words onto the sides of water containers it would change the structure of them. Each word creates a different shape of water crystal.

Words like "Thank You" and "Love" make very well shaped patterns that are healthy structures, and are able to easily penetrate cell walls and hydrate the body, carrying out toxins easily. Negative words would actually break down the very geometries that made the crystals healthy, and would presumably lead to poor health and undesirable emotions.

He found also that thought would affect the shapes of the patterns. A Buddhist monk's blessing provided crystals that were neat and perfect, and some groups of Japanese families were actually able to restore the structure to some Tokyo tap water (it was in really bad shape) by just thinking thankful thoughts to it.

That's the research that is documented in his book, The Message from Water. But Emoto also expanded on the information he had written, adding new insights from his experience and philosophy.

His conclusion is that human beings are special creatures on our planet, because we are able to resonate with anything on the planet, and we are supposed to be the garden keepers, in his words.

When he spoke about "resonating" he took out a tuning fork and made a demonstration. When he sang the note that the fork was tuned to, (A 440) then it began to hum. He even held it up to the microphone he was speaking into and the entire audience could hear.

Then he stopped the sound coming from the tuning fork, sang another note, and it did not vibrate. He even tried singing the note of the tuning fork, just out of tune, and it still did not vibrate.

He explained that in Japanese philosophy, some things are just "attuned to" one another, in a kind of simpatico where they just hum the same note. The special thing about humans he said again was that we are able to use our mind, our neocortex he suggested, to "resonate" on many different levels, with many different creatures and aspects of nature.

That means that we are to be the caretakers of our planet, not its destructors. And something Emoto said in an interview actually correlates to other information interviewees would provide in the future. Supposedly, with the end of the Maya Long Count in 2012, we enter into a different age, one that essentially began with the Fall in the Garden of Eden.

FINDING THE FORCE 1:

Entering into the Age of Aquarius (The Water Bearer) we are supposed to return to our previous position as "like unto the gods," and perhaps water holds the key to that leap. Emoto says:

"I believe that prior to Adam and Eve water itself held the consciousness of God -- that God's intention was put into the medium of water, and that this was used in the creation of Earth and Nature. In other words, all of the information needed for God's Creation was reflected in the water. And then we -- Adam and Eve -- were placed on Earth to be the caretakers for this Creation of God. I believe that water held the consciousness of God until then, but that after the caretakers were placed on Earth, water became an empty vessel to mirror and reflect what was in the heart. It became a container to carry energy and information.

Therefore, since this time, I think water has taken on the quality of simply reflecting the energies and thoughts that it is exposed to; that it no longer has its own consciousness. Water reflects the consciousness of the human race."

If Wolfe was right then that means that perhaps the water in our bodies, combined with our neural networks actually form attractors for certain kinds of experiences. If the actual form of a water crystal with the word "Love" on it has the power to attract electrons who are shopping to manifest love, then every other word, and every other thought would have power too. Water crystals that are attuned to hate or misery would attract and create that show.

It also reminded me of Miguel Ruiz's work, and made me feel the imperative need to go running over to the other side of Omega to go see him and his son speaking. I had not planned on it, but what the heck? I had a free pass for the weekend, courtesy of Omega, and I was convinced that Ruiz had something important to say. Before I left, I went over to speak to Emoto and to hand him a painting. I offered him the painting entitled 'Turtle Island' and when he saw it he laughed and laughed.

His interpreter got a little squeamish, and I asked what was going on. Emoto broke out into English himself, and he explained:

"I was just speaking up in Canada on the West Coast last week and someone handed me this. A Turtle Lodge that a group of Indigenous People have built who share the same vision. Looks just like your painting. Coincidence? Oh and thanks for the painting," Emoto said and smiled.

The flyer he handed me looked exactly like the painting I had just given him. It was definitely a sign I was on my way.

Synchronicity at its finest.

My mouth was hanging open though, because the drawing on the flyer looked exactly like my painting, and this group had actually constructed a Turtle Lodge.

I would later find out t hat the story of Turtle Island was an old deluge story from North America. Like Noah, they had built a ship to float on the rising tides, but in this case a tiny little creature brings up a paw full of earth to start the world again. When the earth was placed on a turtle's back, it began to grow and grow until it became a huge island. Turtle Island.

"Water is a very malleable substance. Its physical shape easily adapts to whatever environment is present. But its physical appearance is not the only thing that changes, the molecular shape also changes. The energy or vibrations of the environment will change the molecular shape of water.

In this sense water not only has the ability to visually reflect the environment but it also molecularly reflects the environment."
-*Masaru Emoto*

"These photographs show the incredible reflections of water, as alive and highly responsive to every one of our emotions and thoughts. It is quite clear that water easily takes on the vibrations and energy of its environment, whether toxic and polluted or naturally pristine.

TRIP 7: DREAM OF THE TURTLE LODGE

I am dreaming of being in the forest again.

FINDING THE FORCE 1:

Thick lush vegetation, but this time I am walking along a path and there is a man with me who I am following. He has on a denim jacket that is very dirty, and he is talking constantly to something in his pockets.

Actually there are multiple somethings. They are baby owls. As we are walking, he notices another one on a ledge of rocks and picks it up and pops it into his pocket. I try to look, but he pulls them away and closes them back up in his jacket.

We keep on walking, and eventually I realize the place is familiar. We are walking through the forests surrounding the Ananda Ashram close to where I was living in the hills of New York, on the west side of the Hudson River. It was so thick and beautiful with moisture and vegetation. The smells of all the life were amazing. Moss, bark, leaves, rotting materials, running rovers, ferns...And the thick sounds of the birds and creatures moving everywhere.

We walked for a very long time and finally came to a strange building. It was shaped with six sides, and was made all of wood clapboard. There was a light coming through the window, and the guy in front of me knocked.

A heavy set older woman with white hair opened the door and smiled.

"What do you have here?"

The man showed her and she smiled.

"We have been looking for one of those! Thank you very much. But you may only bring one inside."

He handed her one, then put another outside on the window ledge. The woman welcomed me in, and asked me to sit down.

FINDING THE FORCE 1

When I looked over though, there was a maze of benches arrayed in line with the six-sided nature of the building. I had a hard time weaving my way through and eventually stopped, just short of the middle.

When I looked up there were two old men sitting there looking back and forth at each other, commiserating. One was very Hindu looking, and was wearing orange colored robes and had very dark skin.

The other was dressed in a white shirt, but had two feathers sticking up from the back of his head. Maybe Eagle Feathers, and he was very wrinkled and old. There wasn't too much doubt he was a Native Elder, but he didn't introduce himself.

They kept nodding their heads and commiserating. It was more than paranoia, I knew for a fact that they were talking about me. And I knew that they were deciding my fate.

It seems that I was to go with the Native, and he opened his hand to me and asked me to come. I thought we were leaving through the door, but as soon as I touched his hand, the reality from inside the structure shifted and disappeared, and there I was inside of a turtle-like water bubble.

Inside this, I could see the structure of the water molecule, and it was a lot like a crystal, and I found the benches that were an obstacle beforehand had marked it out. I just hadn't known what it was.

As my thoughts moved and changed, and my feelings as well, the structure inside this turtle-like water lodge would change too.

I began to realize he was trying to show me that we are affected by our thoughts on more than one level. It actually was shifting the structure of the water as I was thinking and feeling!

Soon the sun rose, and a bright light was coming through a central skylight, a round dome with a dark spot in the middle.

FINDING THE FORCE 1:

The Old One said that that was the symbol for the local sun here by Earth, and that it was going to change its thinking too, and when it did, we would all have to shift with it, the way the benches had shifted with my thoughts.

When we left (through the hole in the center above) I could see many bubbles of light coming towards us. And the lodge I was just inside had a head and feet like a turtle! The turtle was emerging from a vast ocean, rising up and dumping water off its back like a waterfall.

I woke up and began sketching. I was almost used to it now.

TIP 7: Water, ⅔ of our body, responds to Words, Thoughts and Emotions. Our Minds are Powerful. Working with the Breath and Intention we can Maintain Clean, Harmonious Patterns.

CHAPTER EIGHT

Divine Consciousness: Meditation of the Maharishi

"*Knock, And He'll open the door*
Vanish, And He'll make you shine like the sun
Fall, And He'll raise you to the heavens
Become nothing, And He'll turn you into everything."
— *Rumi*

FINDING THE FORCE 1

Albuquerque, NM
June Solstice, 2012

It ends up that I studied with Dominguez for years, trying to unravel the series of strange dreams and interviews included in this novel. I managed to convince him through my sincere efforts that, not only was I a maniac, but one worth teaching shamanism and spiritual practice.

I also pursued yoga as a daily practice, the occasional kung fu, Tibetan Buddhism, herbalism, kabbalah, reiki, homeopathy, farming, and Masonry, not to mention some other standard stuff. I read everything I could read having to do with shamanism and spiritual practice from cultures all over the world.

After all the interviews I had done, I ended up really believing what those people told me, that not only that there was a possibility of taking control of one's own destiny, one's own dream, but that access was gained through intense spiritual practice, cleansing mind, body, spirit, and opening into a state of better cohesion with the Universe at large.

I looked at every different kind of practice I could find, to try to learn what was similar amongst all of them. In their similarities I should find deeper truths, universal ones.

What it really comes down to is that when you have a physical body, it can get badly programmed into a place where it's in a negative feedback cycle, constantly zapping its own neurological system with painful or stressful thoughts, that produce adrenaline, that engage the body in fight of flight mode, to one degree or another, and essentially consume the vital energies of the body until it falls into physical dis-ease, which is nothing but congealed mental dis-ease.

FINDING THE FORCE 1:

How could people escape this bad dream we were all living in? After years of study, I had learned a lot from Don Patricio, and one of the things he told me was like this:

"You see, the Indians didn't have the same cosmology as the white people, the Europeans. We never had a story about being ejected from 'The Garden' by a punishing father. We remained in the garden, at one with the creatures, in a state of harmony and respect for one another. How knowledge takes you away from that is it makes you to believe in a false God. The God of technology. See people nowadays think they are going to fix everything with technology. You break the environment, oh yeah, there's a band aid for that, we can just discover the next big technological fix, and it will make it all better. But you see, eventually, when there are more than 5 billion people on the planet, and all the oceans and air and land are trashed and contaminated and there is war over what's left of the scarce resources that we should all be talking about sharing carefully, you run out of room, and it all starts breaking down.

The only place you can live in Hell is in your own mind, as it's a projection of one's own inner world. The world we have created, subsequently, and as a result of our own inner thoughts and demons, is a world of utter confusion and contamination.

But the belief in the lies that were put forth to us is what led us to this point. And no matter how many Indians once believed in a totally different way of life, it may well have been lost. It just may be that this world is lost. There are too many people, with much too low a level of consciousness to make the proverbial tipping point. Unless something really miraculous happens, we're the next dinosaurs.

But it's not something that has to happen this way. We could change our minds, but it would take a lot of us, or take something like a miracle."

FINDING THE FORCE 1

As I was listening to his rants over the years, which were many and good, I eventually began to protest. I didn't understand why everyone needed to be wiped off the face of the planet.

There were prophecies, and boy Patricio is Prophecy Central, galore about what the end of times was going to look like. He said death and destruction for sure, tsunamis, earthquakes, natural disasters of every kind, a failing economy...

But I also kept on finding prophecies of a new kind of human to be born, a new model so to speak! The warriors of light, children of the rainbow, golden ones, etc. who would carry a different energy, a different way of thinking, and certain abilities that had lain dormant in humans since their Fall from Eden.

I came to believe that there was a way we could carve out a new kind of destiny for ourselves.

So I kept on with every different kind of practice I could to break through to a new level of understanding, and also find those who were in the same state of seeking something, and accomplishing that as well. Because along the way I found plenty of people who totally had fallen by the wayside on their "Path".

But there were signs everywhere of a new level of enlightenment, a desire for awareness amongst people at large.

It seems there are some truths which are applicable to many cultures, and certain secrets that were withheld, stalked, injured, in order to control human's ability to personally connect with their right place in the universe.

If you cannot connect with something outside your own personal reality, which brings good health and inner peace, then it will be difficult to do anything other than suffer. This turns the human body into somewhat a prison cell, and we deal with suffering and depression. And because we

FINDING THE FORCE 1:

have turned into a culture that honors fear and horror, and makes no more than a misogynistic mockery of what otherwise might have been known as Love, we are in a very Hellish place.

There are signs of turning things around. But over the years, I lost faith in producing an actual novel, and came to believe that I would eventually find some other media to distribute the information I had discovered. After a couple of years living in Albuquerque, I made some friends who plugged me into a great guy at the radio station who does work in Bridging Cultures. When I told him about the project, he offered to help us record.

Don Patricio and I began interviewing people on various topics, starting with Sustainability and moving on to Consciousness and Meditation.

The guest speaker for this conversation is the previous attaché to the Maharishi Mahesh Yogi (renowned guru to the Beatles), who first marketed Transcendental Meditation to the Western World.

There are many different meditative techniques, and the best ones all have in common that they drop you into a different level of awareness, of consciousness, one where you are less aware of your own personality, and become aware of something different, something transcendent.

KUNM Recording Studio, June 2012

CH: Good evening. This is the Reverend Courtni Hale here, recording with Lucio Urbano in the studio at KUNM...We will be recording our second talk on Consciousness. I am pleased to have here as guest speakers tonight Vanessa Vidal, Patricio Dominguez and Gordon Eagleheart and to talk about this fascinating subject matter. I'd like to introduce first Vanessa and get a little bit of information on her background.

FINDING THE FORCE 1

VV: Courtni, thank you so much and it's really a pleasure to be here with Gordon and Patricio and yourself. My name is Vanessa Vidal and I am the National Director of the Global Mother Divine Foundation and we offer the Transcendental Meditation program to women in the United States. Really the heart of our organization's mission and our vision is the development of the full potential of a woman's life. And you may ask, why were focused on women, well women you know, the old saying the hand that rocks the cradle rules the earth and we feel that women are the key to really creating a society worthy of the name 'humanity' and an enlightened society free from problems, that women are really the key and the central point that we want to focus on. There is an organization that teaches TM to men and other but we want to focus on women. It's like pulling one leg of a chair, when you pull one leg all the other three legs come along.
And we feel that women are that key leg that will bring everyone with them, because that's the nature of women.

When you teach a woman something she shares it with her friends and family. And so we feel like that's the key. And so our first conversation this evening will be on Consciousness. I have worked with the Transcendental Meditation Organization since 1971 so for over 35 years, more than that and I have traveled all over the world, but right now I am the National Director of the organization offering TM to women in the United States.

CH: Wow, thank you so much for sharing your background. I am sure that will help everyone understand how important it is to listen to the message. We also Gordon Eagleheart with us too, who is a carrier of the Toltec traditions, and I'd like to introduce him.

GE: Yes, glad, wonderful to be here. What I do is I guide others in becoming free of their domestication. So it's very similar to what Vanessa was speaking about. Why was it that I do not have access to this source of my consciousness? In the Toltec traditions we describe that as our domestication. And we are steered away from that ownership. It's just been going on from generation to generation. And the Toltec

FINDING THE FORCE 1:
Traditions help us to guide ourselves to the recovery and the truth of what we truly are. And in that regard we are very much in alignment - we do meditations as well and are very much in alignment with discovering the truth of who we are and how we are using our power of consciousness and how we are actually stewards of the dream we are creating in this moment.

CH: Super. On my right here I have Don Patricio Dominguez. And let's see...

PD: Good Evening. I am Patricio Dominguez and I have been part of the Consciousness process since I was a child, I am Native American and so I was brought into consciousness as a practice and a study, you might say by elder's mandate. I was chosen at 5 years old to be on this road of consciousness to serve the community as a healer and troubleshooter for the community. Basically I was supposed to gain enough wisdom and knowledge basically to help the people of the community solve just about any problem that could come their way. So consequently I had to apply myself to pretty much every aspect of human life psychology, physiology, you name it. I had to heal not only mind body, but soul.

CH: Well the first question that I would like to introduce is you know, now that we established in part one basically what Consciousness is, we are in this place where we know that we want to go somewhere by developing our consciousness but where do we go with it and what effect does it have on our life when achieve some better or higher state of consciousness? Can we have Vanessa first?

VV: You know, the beautiful thing about our consciousness is, and we were having a discussion before we went on the air, it is quite literally the basis of everything. Every thought we have happens within our consciousness. How effective that thought is depends on the quality and power of our consciousness. Our thoughts turn into actions which turn into achievements and fulfillments. So it's literally the basis of everything in our individual lives.

FINDING THE FORCE 1

The purpose of developing your consciousness is to really make use of more of your mental potential. We are only using a very small percentage of our mental potential, maybe less than 12% if we are Einstein. So how do we develop that mental potential so that our thoughts are fully powerful…They are at their full level of power and our actions are therefore at their full level of not just power but in tune with Natural Law so that our actions don't violate any natural law, they are in tune with nature.

So in order to have that happen we have to have fully developed consciousness. That is actually the state of enlightenment. And Maharishi described enlightenment as the most naturally normal state of life. If you are not living full enlightenment and you are not using your full brain power your full mental potential, your full consciousness then actually you are living less than your potential, less than what life has given you.

CH: Wow, I am just in a happy place listening to you speak about it that way and I hope that people get a chance to listen to these words of advice. Gordon?

GE: I'd like to move into the root of consciousness. The essence of consciousness, the very essence, the root of it, begins at perception. So it's, at that moment, one can perceive something and something that it is not. What many of us do not realize is that consciousness is abundant in the universe. Consciousness, if you look at a single celled organism, like an amoeba, it can perceive what food is, and what food is not. It has that root essence of consciousness, the white blood cells, they can perceive that which is something which is to be attacked in order to sustain life in the human body.

So the very very root of consciousness is profoundly large and beyond our imagining. The way we begin to create harmony in our consciousness is also being able to, how do we go about communicating with all the consciousness that within our vessel. Yes our consciousness

FINDING THE FORCE 1:

resides in our thinking patterns, but that's a manifestation of our intention.

What many of us are struggling with is that we are not aware of where our intent is, where our attention is, and we have been placing our attention in ways that's not in harmonious with the truth of what we are.

In harvesting the realization of what our intention is and how it is communicated throughout our entire vessel, and also in relationship to the universe, through that process we become clearer of who we are and how we are related to everything else, and through that communion clarity emerges and the full potential of who and what we are shows up.

CH: Thank you. That reminds me so much of the teachings of Miguel Ruiz. Which makes a lot of sense because you are carrying that tradition. I remember speaking with him one time he said something so concise.

As attention goes so follows energy.

You know? And whatever you are putting your attention on, like you are saying, is kind of a preconceived little spot in the universe you are perceiving everything from and we can use our energy in an intentional way, right, and focus on something positive.

PD: I'd like to interject some things into the conversation. Because consciousness has been something that I have put my attention on for a really long time, I started deliberating on what really constituted the difference between c and higher c. Higher c is a term and even a phrase that has been bandied about but nobody really clearly has been able to speak about what is the difference between c and higher c. At what point does the human being express or how do you qualify that a human being has reached higher consciousness.

Because if you're just c and you say well um I have higher consciousness because I am aware of the deeper aspects of life and I have been told that

FINDING THE FORCE 1

Mother Earth is a living being, and I'm aware of these things. The question is are you aware of it because this has been brought to your attention or are you aware of it because you actually had the mental capacity to perceive it?

That I think is the difference between consciousness and higher consciousness. Having the ability to perceive things beyond ordinary consciousness. Because everybody can be consciousness of the highest knowledge on the planet if it's taught to them but to have actually perceived it form their own resources, to have actually had the capacity to perceive this very profound insight into the workings of the universe requires a higher consciousness. And really what I'd like to talk about is that higher consciousness. Because it is a better functioning, a higher order functioning of the human being.

And it's not, it's not naturally born, it has to be developed. It's a lot like a musical talent. Even though you might have the ear for music until you have actually been taught the difference between do-re-mi-fa-so-la-ti-do you really don't really understand how to work with it even though you have been introduced to that it takes a little development. Higher c is something that is not only a capacity, it is also a working with and developing of those capacities.

That's what I wanted to kind of talk about is this odd thing called higher consciousness. I wanted to throw that on the table and I'll give my perspective on it and I'll listen to see if somebody else has another perspective on it.

CH: Yeah, it's really important to understand that there's a whole spectrum of c from one state to another, from waking to dreaming, and all these things are Vibrational and so the analogy to music is a wonderful one, and because you have octaves of music and sound and light and I think our c is a little bit like a radio where we can tune in to different levels and layers of things and what are we trying to tune into and how and why is probably a really great question. Would it be all right for Vanessa to go ahead?

FINDING THE FORCE 1:

PD: I was hoping someone was just going to chime in!

VV: Well, I'm ready to chime in because I love what you said. I think that normal consciousness that we normally think, you are either awake, you are either awake in your waking state of consciousness or in your in your dream state of consciousness or in your sleep state of consciousness, these are the three levels of consciousness that most people live in. And they don't know anything else. They don't know any other higher consciousness. They don't know anything else; they don't know any other higher consciousness.

Now the interesting thing about c is that you can put someone in a room and they can be awake and you can measure their EEG and their metabolic rate. And without ever seeing them you can tell whether they are awake, they are asleep or they are dreaming. Because there is literally a unique physiological and brain wave state to each state of consciousness.

Now what we see, when people practice TM and they transcend the finest level of thinking to this unbounded, blissful state of their inner consciousness is that that also has a unique style of physiological and mental functioning.

And then beyond that, so they experience it when they meditate, they come out into waking state and that style of functioning fades in the physiology and they meditate again, they come out and that style of Transcendental consciousness, this 4th major state of consciousness starts to fade in activity. But what eventually starts to happen is that the longer they practice, and it's not a difficult practice, it's actually a very simple process, that state of T consciousness that 4th state of unique consciousness, starts to not fade away.

Now this now, is now a 5th unique style of brainwave and physiological functioning, a 5th state of consciousness. If you put someone in a room and they are in this state of what we call Cosmic Consciousness you can tell it by looking at their brainwaves and their metabolic rate.

Now what happens to a person that starts to function in these higher states of consciousness is that they bring more to the table. They bring more of their inner potential to the table. They use more of their minds. Their bodies become healthier. Their mind body coordination improves. They really start to live more of their full potential.

This to us, and to me is the higher levels of c that you are talking about. And quite literally they are scientifically measurable. Which is so fascinating. It's not a matter of do I believe I am in Cosmic Consciousness? Do I feel like I transcended?

No. I can show you that you absolutely did, and that style of functioning in the physiology is incredibly healthy. It's a natural style of functioning and if you are not using that then you are living with dis-ease in your physiology. A lack of ease. A lack of fully functioning physiology and brain functioning.

GE: Yes, I'd like to just jump in here. That's all great. It's very much in alignment with when I work with people. One of the things that showed up for me, the word I use is realization, to help people recognize the distinction between an intellectual knowing and having something become real in their experience.

VV: Exactly.

GE: And so in the journey I always have people asking, saying the same thing, when am I going to get there? My answer is always, When does a tree know it's a tree? Does the tree stop growing? Does it stop producing leaves? Or does it continue to produce new leaves each year?

And consciousness is very much like that. I mean we are no different, we are life. We are life. The amazing thing about humanity is the potential we have in our consciousness.

FINDING THE FORCE 1:

We are incredibly conscious being and we have a symbiotic relationship with the entire universe through our consciousness. The power of our consciousness. We actually provide awareness to the universe of itself. That's how strong and powerful we are.

And the journey to that discovery is starting to recognize that within ourselves. So this higher state is simply part of that journey and you're moving along, we're growing just like a little tree. At first we are a little stem coming out and as we grow we start to develop the awareness and start to see the potential of what we are.

But the journey never ends, it's not like you finally say one day, now I'm aware, now I am an enlightened individual and it's all done. There is always another door, another gate to go through. SO the journey is a continuous and beautiful one. The one thing I wanted to point out is that it becomes more joyous and more beautiful and the farther you continue to go along. You've just got a greater view.

CH: Yeah, and I suppose with the kind of practice that Vanessa is talking about you begin to shift your neurology and your thoughts patterns and your awareness so that you are more and more in that 5th state of consciousness.

I like to think about yoga a lot and one of the things I think about is that it means yoking, and yoking what to what – yoking the diving to the body so that we can be both at the same time.

Another thing we like to talk about a lot is this paradigm shift that's coming and maybe we could talk about the collective consciousness that we are trying to develop. A lot of us are healers and medicine people or ministers of one variety or another you know we go into a lodge and we pray together and we form something beautiful an unique which I'd like to think is a collective consciousness

FINDING THE FORCE 1

PD: Actually it is. A collective consciousness is just that it's when you have a collective of individuals that share a consciousness. But as Gordon pointed out that's really a spectrum. At every level you can have a collective consciousness because if you have a group of people in a room and you have a lot of people who are at the you might say 5th level of consciousness, or which as I like to call awake ++ then you have a collective consciousness at awake ++ and its going to be a very profound situation because now people have something to connect about or talk about or relate about that is an order above what the ordinary consciousness can talk about.

Again using art as an example if you look at a piece of art and you are not really an artist you will see the beauty of it at whatever level you have the capacity for. But if you have been working in that medium and you know a lot more about the technique and the details of that style then when you look at it and see what everybody else is seeing but then another level so you can see a deeper beauty in that piece of work.

And the same is true for having higher order of consciousness and being on planet Earth. If you have a higher level of consciousness, Earth is even more beautiful than it is when you are just awake, the beauty of mother earth at Awake + is even more incredible, if you can believe that, than what it is at just Awake.

People in those states, in any state can have collective consciousness. Unfortunately a collective consciousness, I fell can happen at lower levels.

VV: I just want to say, I am so fascinated by this field, this matter of collective consciousness. I just think it's one of the most interesting subjects that you could ever look at. Because you can absolutely influence it for the good. That's the thing that's really remarkable about it. It doesn't matter how bad it is, if enough people are living in that higher consciousness, they can affect it.

I want to give you some examples.

FINDING THE FORCE 1:

In the 1960's when the Maharishi first started teaching TM, he predicted that when 1% of any city, any population, learned TM, that crime would go down. And that's exactly what we saw around the world. And we've repeated this. This is the most extensive sociological research study that has ever been done, ever. And the results are actually, you can't argue them.

The p value is so small it could not have happened for any other reason but that a set number of people, making their own brain waves coherent, together in a city, enough of them, creating individually coherence for themselves, but when there's enough of them they can have an influence on the entire group, on the society.

There are some things in science where when 1% of the atoms in a light become coherent, then the entire light becomes a laser. When 1% of the cellular matter in DNA becomes coherent and start to function in an orderly manner that's enough to change the entire functioning of the cell, it's the same in chemistry, it's the same in every science, so we are nothing other than Nature. So when we have enough people functioning in a coherent way in themselves, and there are enough of them, then we can, on a dime, transform this society. So if there's enough of us doing, or creating these experiences if higher consciousness, creating coherence in our brains, you don't even have to do anything other than that, to transform this society.

CH: Wow. Well I can hardly wait to talk more, our next segment is going to be on meditation, and hopefully we can get into some of the scientific information you are talking about and delve a little deeper into that. I want to wrap up now and thank you everybody so much, thank you to everyone at the station here who has volunteered their time, Gordon, Patricio and Vanessa, and good night for the Monday Night talk for now.

FINDING THE FORCE 1

TRIP 8: DREAM OF THE "HIT" MEN

Albuquerque, NM 2012

They are coming to take me away again. This time, they are being a little bit rough, and I can't speak. My throat is clogged, cut off, and I can only hack and sputter some gravelly grunty sounds. When I do try though, they push harder and mock me. They think it's funny that I can't even talk.

Like opening a bottle of fine wine that smells of vinegar.

They had expected something more.

In the dream, I am being moved forward through this tightly carpeted hallway, with dim lights running along the top of the walls, like tiny emergency lights. It's a long straight hallway, with rooms on either side, and it smells like schools do, a certain kind of new carpet smell or mixed with industrial flavors of sanitizer, mixed with old paint.

And I can't see anything, but I think I knew where I was.

FINDING THE FORCE 1:

Why do these guys always come and take me away? What's the big deal about?

It's the tenth, at least of this series of dreams, ultra vivid, where I am being kidnapped or chased or drug around by some kinda thought police, who have determined that I am a serious danger to their status quo, and every once in a while, I need some serious management. Ones in boats, ones in stairways, ones who tracked me, stalked me, eventually killed a part of me that was once my personality.

I guess I didn't need it anymore anyhow.

But now these big snickerdoodle thugs in shiny suits kinda kick open a door on the left, and it's all dark in there.

Oh no no nonooo. I am so not going in there. Forget it boys.

I start to really buck pretty hard, start to really make off in the other direction, but before I know it, they push me in.

You know how it goes after that. The door has to slam and I have to kick it and beat it for a while, no luck.

I hear more laughing, but, good natured. There are other people in the room! And there's sounds coming from all over.

When my eyes adjust and I can see a room a bit, I see there is a large window of plate glass in the middle of it. I can see a smog on the other side of it, and I am afraid that that think smoky thing is going to get me, devour me, eat me up!

But then I see there are others, and they are smoking. Well, it's as if the waves in the air are penetrating them, then coming back out again as something distinct and unique, but still smoke.

FINDING THE FORCE 1

They are all sitting in chairs, one is an old time cat with a decent hat and a smile. He's playing an upright base. And tapping his foot.

There are a couple guys on rhythm, so smooth, so natural, and they are great. But they are totally smokin'. Pun intended.

On my right is some kind of horn player, a trumpet, but soft soft, smooth.

And then, when I am taken in by the smog myself, after I pass through a momentary terror, I am OK, and I can hear them all, and interact with them. On the other side of the plate glass where there was once a smog, there is a guy with a mike and earphones.

He's saying,

"Hey Courtni. Are you gonna sing or not? Are we here to sing, or are we not?"

And everybody laughs real hard in a great way,

And I start to sing.

And there were sparkling spots in the smog, glittering lights, when all made our music together.

TIP 8: Meditation is Key to Quieting the Mind and Allowing us to Find our Right Place in the Universe.

CONCLUSION:
Check Out Finding The Force, Events and Classes.
www.FindingTheForce.com
Sequel to this novel is full of Teachings and more wild adventures in New Mexico and beyond.

FINDING THE FORCE 1:

Made in the USA
Las Vegas, NV
14 November 2021